CHAOS

Juliet Holmes

Contents

▯ ▯ ▯ ▯ ▯ ▯ ▯ ▯

"VIOLET, tell me to stop and I'll stop" the feeling of his soft lips igniting flames throughout my body, my lower half becoming warmer every second I felt the delicacy of his touch.

"Enzo" I couldn't bring myself to say stop, simply because I didn't want him to. I wanted his hands roaming over my body while he held my neck thrusting into me. The erection I feel on my thigh made my mind wonder off. Pinching my hip I moaned lowly when he hooked my legs around his waist.

"That's not telling me to stop amore" removing my shirt over my head his lips latched onto my swollen nipples, my hands shot in the softness that was his black hair.

"That's because you can't tell me to stop can you, you don't want me to" the deepness of his voice making my back arch, my chest meeting his.

"Tell me what you want"

When I accepted his offer I was already screwed, why not sink further down into his world.

"Fuck me Enzo"

□□□□□□

□□□□ ever I was close to his heart, when he showed me how venerable he was, he'd push me away as if I was dust on his shoulder. Something that wasn't supposed to be permanent turned into exactly that. Corrupting my mind, my body, my life. Enzo wasn't good for me, he was like a drug you got hooked on and couldn't get off of, when you did you went back to get more.

Enzo Romano's possessiveness over me only made me want to play his games back.

"Just his dancer" he says as he continues to let the other girls dance on his lap.

Teasing him was dangerous and could get me into so much trouble or punishments as he calls it, though I couldn't care less. Enzo wasn't going to toy with me because he felt like it. Enzo would only bring me nothing but chaos but I wanted it, every part of him. Enzo was the chaos in my life, he brought out sides to me I didn't believe I had.

□□□□

□□□□□□□□□□ was a word to describe Violet, the way her body moved on top of mine instantly making me hard. When I needed a dance she was there, she wanted to know what troubled me but I only kept quiet. Her ass rotating down on me, her brown eyes watching me colored in lust. Dipping her head into my neck, she was my first dancer who got to touch me like this. Her nails lightly scratching the back of my neck tugging my hair until I looked into her eyes.

Violet had me trapped.

She wasn't ready for the secrets that came with my life. She'd only be scared of it all, the moment she stepped foot through that door and placed her self in my lap.

Violet became mine.

The second I brought to my life style she would only cry to be let go from the sleepless nights that came with it.

□ □ □

□

□□□□□ was what the street was at this time, dark and cold there was no light. All streets lights broken or flickering all that was giving me light was the small shop with the illuminating colored sign. Holding the trench coat in my hands knocking on the metal door, the small peep hole opened revealing two hazel colored eyes. A tall dark tanned skinned man walked out, overpowering muscles poking out of his black shirt. He stood looking at the sides of the streets, the silver rhinestones framing my breast to the matching heels.

"Enzo Romano please" I didn't know who Enzo was but they said he owned the club along with the girls inside. The man checked my I.D before realizing I was knew he unlocked the door allowing me in.

The smell of whiskey and different scents of cologne mixed in the air with the dark red lights blaring around the room. The girls doing what they do best enchanting the rich men, gold watches on their wrist, hair perfectly styled and jaws sharp as ever.

Some married, some newly divorced. The rules were not to touch the girls without permission, one man hadn't listened to that rule currently being thrown out behind me. A gorgeous woman approached me her blonde hair pulled into a ponytail high on her head, the woman smiled hugging me. Her long legs covered in small glitter dust showing off her toned body.

"Valerie" she stuck her hand out smiling, passing all the men looking at my body like a piece of meat we entered the black door containing the rest of the dancers.

"Violet" the back of the chair read next to her own.

"Today will be your first day here, they aren't allowed to touch you with your consent, you dance the whole time until the light shuts off." she said before fixing her lipstick, smacking her lips together she stood up spinning around adorning herself.

"You're up" she said fluffing out my hair, throwing small amounts of glitter on my chest to my legs. Leading me to the back of the stage threw the curtains men could be seen staring at the pole waiting impatiently.

The dim color of the room changed, not being able to see the men anymore I only focused of the illumination of the single pole waiting for me. My heels clicked against the floor, the single light raining down on me. Whistles and compliments flooding my ears, the green paper flowing on the stage already and I hadn't even done anything yet.

The cold metal of the pole hit my hot skin as I slowly slid down keeping my legs closed teasing them. Opening my legs, low curses heard from each man before I winked at them closing them once again. Now on my back, leaving my legs closed my hands ran up to my breast squeezing them in my hands. The reflection of the rhinestones on the glass stage only showing my body more. Turning on my knees I arched my back on the center of the stage.

Directly in the middle of the booth sat Enzo Romano watching me intensely. His legs opened for me, his dark black hair neatly falling on his forehead. Tattoos easy to see through the white fitted shirt, he leaned his forearms on his knees smirking at me with his pink lips. Returning a smile I moved closer to him reaching a hand out for him, cupping his jaw he growled lowly when I turned away.

Spreading my knees on the stage I ran my hands down my body stopping where they desired me the most all the way back up to my stomach, to my neck where I lightly choked my self hearing the cheers.

His deep blue eyes, taking in every inch of my curves. His strong arms still on his knees tilting his head to see what I was going to do next. Silver rings on his left and two on the right along with the decorated tattoo with the letter R.

Dangerous was what he spoke, though I didn't know much about him I could tell Enzo was a man of high power. Moving back to the pole I spun around until my leg hooked around it sliding down again I landed in the split feeling the money graze my body onto the floor. Loud cheering around me from the both men and women who I had noticed to the side of me.

The light on top of me cut off leaving the men to wonder who I was, the small passage for me to go Valerie handed me the trench coat congratulating me on how well I did before we reached the room.

"I'm telling you, I've never seen Enzo so lost in someone's dance" she said sitting down.

"Are you sure that was your first show because holy shit, you had me turned on" I laughed nodding, it was my first show but it wasn't my first time dancing on a pole. I took a lot of classes before I started this job.

"Literally the hottest dancer here, don't tell the others" she whispered to me.

"Don't lie to the poor girl and get her hopes up Val" our heads turned to another dancer, red rhinestones on her body. Her black hair flowing down to her back. Giving both of us a fake smile we returned.

"I'm sure Enzo didn't like it that much" she sat flipping her hair. Her chair read Helena, she fixed the mascara on her eye lashes.

Another woman came from the same door but this time she wasn't a bouncer. Helena stood up cheerfully knowing who the woman was but she passed her coming to me.

"Mr. Romano would like to see you upstairs now" was all she said before leaving. Valerie squealed behind me and Helena huffed leaving.

"What?"

"That's new, Enzo doesn't request anyone other than Helena" Valerie said.

"What do you mean request?"

"Helena was his personal dancer before he kinda stopped asking for her" she showed me to the long stair way.

"Not sure exactly why but here we are."

"Just go up and knock, good luck" she kissed my cheek leaving me to stare up at the dark hallway.

The sounds of my heels grew louder as the loud crowd died out only to be canceled out by my heavy breathing.

The tinted windows not allowing me to see inside I knocked softly waiting for the right to enter.

Whatever Enzo wanted with me wouldn't be good for me at all. The power that radiated off of him even just by sitting wasn't going to be easy to work with and for. Eyes screaming murderous but his features unbelievably attractive, that's what he wanted you to fall for before you noticed that he could kill you.

"Come in."

□

/ □□□□□□□ 1 □□□□□□□□ ?

▯ ▯ ▯

□□

□ □□□□□ leather welcomed my body, the coldness of the room wasn't anything compared the burning of my body as he watched me from his seat. Arms crossed showing off the bulging muscles and tattoos, Enzo ran a hand over his stubble on his jaw. Scanning his eyes over the rounds of my breast to the curves of my hips.

"Violet" his voice deep as I expected along with the Italian accent slipping off his tongue. "You're late."

"I got a little.. lost" I lied, it took me five minutes before I built up the courage to knock.

Standing up he made his way over to me. The black belt around his pants facing me, holding my jaw lightly he lifted my head up to meet his empty gaze.

"I don't like it when people are late"

"Then you should give better directions" sinister smile was what it was, appearing on his lips he leaned down to my ear. His fingers grazing up my exposed thigh stopping at the rhinestones.

"I'd watch the way you speak to me tesoro." Sending shivers down my spine on how close he was, the pleasing scent of his mixing with the coconut scent of my own.

Hearing me go silent he returned to his seat. "There was something you needed?" picking up a beige file he ran his eyes down the white paper before placing it down.

"You have a beautiful body Violet" he started. My eyes wondering to the unbuttoned top of his shirt.

Focus Violet.

"Thank you."

"A body that drives me towards you, one that I wouldn't like anyone else to see" I squirmed in my seat a bit as he took in my body, drinking my body up with his eyes.

"Where is this going sir?" Something in his eyes flashed before it was wiped away once more with darkness.

"I haven't had a personal dancer in months, the last.. doesn't intrigue me" he stood up.

"Not like you do"

"With all do respect Mr. Romano, that's not what I signed up do" I was only doing this for my mother, once I had enough to pay for her treatments I would quit.

"There's a lot in it for you Violet." he faced me.

Walking back towards me his tall frame standing over me looking at me sitting on the couch, my legs crossed over the other.

"I'm sorry Mr. Romano" I stood up, my chest brushing his. Cursing my self feeling my nipples harden I'm sure he could feel them, leaving no space between us.

"I'd pay you five times more than what you earn now" That would help so much, but I just.. dammit.

Bracing myself I went to the door ready to open it when it shut in my face. His body sending goosebumps all over my body. The mint of his breath hitting my neck. His chest on my back his arm still holding the door closed. I kept my eyes close trying to calm the heat that I felt as he spoke.

"Think about it Violet"

□

"□□□□ did he want from you?" Helena said a bit disgusted.

"That isn't for you to know" I moved past her, she grabbed my arm.

"Enzo would never ask for a dance from anyone but me just know I'm his favorite, his only dancer."

"I guess you're lucky then, because I said no" her faced formed into one of confusion.

"You said no to him" she asked in more of a question.

"I'm nobodies private dancer, why do you care so much" I knew she was probably the dancer he was talking about when he said he got bored of his last.

Helena was beautiful, but her attitude towards anyone who mentioned Enzo ruined her personality.

"Good because I am his only dancer" I yanked my arm from her, she weirdly growled at me sounded more like a howl.

"Helena" Enzo said behind her, her attitude switched into one of a preppy high school student, skipping over to him she smiled.

"Do you need a dance Enzo?" she said saying it loudly so I could hear her as if I wasn't one foot away from them.

"No, go entertain someone downstairs" he shooed her off, my arms behind my back waiting for the conversation to finish when she pushed past me.

Enzo came over me, pulling my towards him his the coldness of his rings on my bare hip. My hand laying on his arm keeping my balance in my heels.

"Mr. Romano I don't think"-

"You'll give into me Violet soon" he said like a promise, going to respond something on the side of his hip poked me.

When I looked a gun sat on his side.

"Why do you have a gun?"

"Don't ask questions you already know the answer to tesoro" the hall was dark, no one allowed up here unless requested by Enzo. My back hitting the wall behind up he lifted the gun to my face. Truth was I didn't know why he had a gun, maybe because this place was filled with creeps and constantly drunk men.

Taking it he placed it on my lips making them part for him, tracing it down to the beginning of my breast down my stomach. Brining it back up to my lips, my eyes never left his. The hard weapon staying at its place on my lips. I should be terrified that a gun was so close to my body probably one that was loaded.

He kept his eyes on mine watching my chest rise, something in his eyes telling me it was safe. Tucking the gun back in his pocket when his phone rang. Loosing the feeling of his body so close to mine.

"Enjoy the rest of your night Violet"

□

□□ mother's coughing could be heard from the streets, her forehead beaded with drops of sweat. I made way more than enough to buy her medicine for the month.

"Violet, the fat man came today about the rent" she swallowed the next two pills. I had totally forgotten about the rent, by now the money was already spent so she had something to eat. Though the food was enough for the both of us, I made sure she ate first.

"I'll pay it when I get the money" I said letting her food cool down before giving it to her.

"Are you not going to eat?" I shook my head.

"I'm not hungry" kissing her forehead I helped her tie her vanishing brown curls on the top of her head.

"I'll be down stairs okay" I turned on her favorite show before closing her door slightly. Laying on the couch the pillow comforted my head.

Loud banging on our door made me jump up, opening it our landlord Daniel stood with his arms crossed over his stomach.

Storming inside he pushed me out the way. "I told you to fucking pay me or you'd be out on your ass along with your mother" he took the glass cup on the wall shattering it on the floor just as he always did when I was late with his money.

"I need more time" he laughed darkly taking out a piece of paper.

"This says you pay me the last day of every month Violet, do you think I'm playing with you" Daniel was short maybe two inches taller than I was, light brown skin with soulless eyes. He made sexual comments to me when I moved in here.

Coming over to me he twisted my wrist. "You can always pay for it in other ways" I felt disgusted in his touch.

"I would never sleep with you, piece of shit" my hand came in contact with his cheek, his skin now red with my hand print.

"You're going to pay for that you bitch, either you give me my money tomorrow or I'll throw you out myself."

"I would hate for something to happen to your poor mother while you weren't home" with that he shut the door hard making the photo of my father fall and shatter.

Broken glass just surrounding my feet, my phone on the side of it all. I reached for it lingering my finger on the call button. Accepting this would help both my mother and I, we needed this, the money. I would do anything for her.

The phone being picked up on the second ring.

"Violet" he sounded tired and in the middle of something.

"I'll do it"

□

/ □ □□□ □□ □□□□ □□□□□ □□□□□□□□ □□□! □□□□ □□□ □□□□□ □□□ □□□□□ □ □□ □□□□□□□□

□ □ □ □ □

□□□

□□□□□□□ sat with her toned legs crossed over the other, her brown skin untouched by the dark sin that was playing in my thoughts looking at her in that dress. The memory of her lips on my gun came rushing back, I hate to admit it but it was all I could think about until I got her phone call.

The question on why she accepted a few hours after she made it clear it wasn't something she wanted, pushed to the back of my thoughts when she cleared her throat.

"How exactly would this work Mr. Romano?" I took the file off of my desk handing it to her.

"You'd still come to work of course but you'd only tend to me, I'd call you when needed and you'd have access up here at anytime unless I warn you otherwise" she opened the beige file reading through it.

"How long would this go on for?"

"Until either one of decides to call it off" Getting rid of Helena wasn't easy, she insisted that she could do better but her lips drowned in red lipstick didn't do it for me anymore. I got bored of my dancers easily after a week of them signing the contract.

No one has been able to change that.

"You'd make way more than you do now, I'd pay you even when you aren't dancing for me" her eyes widen.

"Why would you do that, not saying that I'm not accepting the offer but"-

"Let's just say, somethings are worth paying over ten thousand for" I scanned over her body. Her sinister lips ready to say something before she stopped herself.

"If you don't mind me asking, does this mean I'd be your only dancer?" she asked with questionable eyes.

"Yes, you'd be the only one allowed to touch me, dance on me and the first I'd let feel my body during your dances" Past dancers were only allowed to move their hips around on me, I didn't want that anymore I needed more.

Seeing Violet on that stage knowing her body so damn well, dragging more attention to her performance. Watching her cup her breast for only my imagination to run wild on what was hiding beneath the tight white dress she wore.

"I have one rule Mr. Romano."

"Call me Enzo tesoro, and what is that rule" she stood up handing me contract she signed.

"You're allowed to touch me, but you aren't allowed to kiss me" she pushed the curls off of her shoulder.

Pinching down on her chin, her lips parted. "Is that so amore?" flashing bits of hunger in her eyes.

"No kissing Enzo that's the rule."

"Then so be it then" Silence fell between us, I would say it subconsciously moved to her smooth skin but that would be a lie. Her body reacted softly as the pads of my fingers fell upon her exposed thigh.

"When do I start?" her voice came out low.

"That is up to you tesoro, but I must warn you" I pushed her down to the couch behind her, holding my arm up I leaned closer to her lips.

"I'm an impatient man."

"Then I guess you can wait can't you?" she got up smoothly turning on her heels.

"I have a show in five minutes, you'll be there to watch me won't you Enzo."

"I wasn't kidding when I said the only person you dance for is me Violet, or do I have to show you" the playful demeanor dropped when she saw that I was serious.

Holding her jaw, her body heat rose against mine. "Do you want me to show you?, because I'll be more than happy too" she shook her head no.

"No I understand" The windows in my office were tinted also sound proof, it was impossible for anyone to try to listen to anything when the door was closed.

"Good girl, I'll send your first check over tonight" Intriguing me not only with her body but her mind, it was clear as day that Violet was a submissive brat. Though I knew she wasn't ready for any of that, I only messed with her just get the small reactions.

Watching her finally shut the door my phone rang.

"What is it?" I fixed my shirt taking a seat.

"You've got to be way more excited to hear from me" Damien said through the phone. The glass window giving me the view of downstairs, Helena preforming in the private areas. Looking around for Violet she wasn't to be found.

"You seem to mistaken me for someone who cares for your life." Violet walked out of the room with a change of clothes before getting stopped by one of the bouncers.

"That is no way to speak to me dear brother, quite frankly I'm hurt" At this point I wasn't listening to anything he was saying, Violet tried to move away from the man twice her size but he didn't let her.

"I just wanted to let you know, I'll be there tomorrow " Hanging up before he said anything else I went down stairs.

Moving Violet behind me, the bouncer stunk of alcohol. He had to be new because I didn't know his name, his eyes droopy staring at her behind me.

"Outside side" I snapped at the other bouncer Garrett to take the drunken man outside.

"Did he touch you?" She responded with a small no that came out in a whisper.

"No he didn't, what are you going to do with him?" everyone around us including Helena watching us.

"What did I say about asking questions you know the answer to?"

"Don't ask them" bending down to her ear so she was the only one who heard my next words.

"Good girl"

□

□□□□□□□ in back of the building silenced by my gun in the pathetic man in front of me. I saw the red twisting marks on her wrist even when she told me he hadn't hurt her. His wrist tied behind him on the chair the one light of the back giving us the clear view of the tears running from his eyes.

"You know Enzo, it's way more fun when the scream for mercy" Mariano said next to me.

Taking out his knife he put pressure on the man's neck, he pleaded for mercy. Mercy wasn't something Mariano was good at giving. He left them with slash marks on their chest, with a carved M on their backs.

The man's words coming out muffled by my gun.

"But I'm not sure that he's the one who caused the harsh marks on her, those look about a day old."

"Take care of this" I wiped my gun off on his shirt. Leaving someone with Mariano and a knife was like leaving a child in a candy store, they had their fun.

Entering the door Helena hooked her leg around my thigh. "I miss you Enzo" pushing her off I went upstairs with her following, Violet looking at us furrowing her eyebrows before averting her eyes.

"Helena you're not allowed up here." Helena's tainted lips now colored in dark purple matching her cloth less outfit on her body.

"Enzo, just give me another chance" After letting Helena go from the contract after three months she's been bothering me to take her back. She wants a relationship with me like she could handle what came along with my life, but that was the problem no one could. It only got them killed or it broke them to be with me, to come to peace with my demons that keep me up at night remember every crucial detail of the first time I watched blood drain out of a lifeless body.

"What don't your understand, I'm done with you" it sounded like I was talking to her like an object but Helena didn't care, I could speak to her like shit and she'd still beg for me to make her my personal dancer.

"So you're choosing that bitch over me seriously?" I snapped my head to her, the color draining from her eyes.

Taking her by her neck she gasped. "I'm choosing Violet over you because she's better than you Helena, she turns me on and you don't simple as that."

"Now go down stairs and do what you're getting paid for before I kill you" I tapped the gun on her skull.

Running down the steps with fear in her eyes.

That's exactly what I meant.

A small threat like that wouldn't prepare anyone for the bigger ones to come.

"I never liked her" Valerie said coming up the stairs.

"Relax I'm not here for you, you're brother requested I meet him in his room" Damien and Valerie had an off and on relationship. Valerie was the only dancer who truly lived in our lifestyle because of him, he tried his hardest to get her away from it but it was easier said than done.

"Back together again?" she rolled her eyes.

"He apologized."

"He did the last time and you almost didn't forgive him" I heard her laugh from down the hall.

"I love him Enzo, I still hate him for disappearing for two months without telling me." she said closing the door to his room. Looking down at the tables, Violet laughed with one of the other girls. Her smile leaving everyone around her speechless, she pushed the curls away from her face. The light fell onto her eyes brightening them.

My phone ringing snapped me out of the trance.

"What?"

"It's about your father Enzo"

□

/ □□□□□□□□□ □□□□□□□ □□ □□□□ □□□□□□□□!!

□ □ □ □

□□

□

□□□□□□□ for Enzo to open the door or give me access in the cold hall made me hug my arms around my body, it was midnight and after the large amount of money sent to my phone I was able to pay off rent for this month. Enzo called me at the mist of leaving the building.

The door cracked opened, entering it shut behind me, lifted up my legs enclosed around his waist. I didn't get time to register everything before he was sitting on the couch with me on his lap. The smack that came upon my ass was hard and loud.

"What do you want me to do Enzo?" his eyes looked tired of everything. He was locked up here all day, different men dressed well flooded up the stairs into this room.

"For one I want you to ride me, but not yet" his hands went down to my hips, his voice dying down an octave making it sound huskier than it already was. My subconscious had my mind wondering off at the thought of riding Enzo. Removing the dirty ideas from my mind I responded.

"You know we can't do that, the rules."

"The rule was that I couldn't kiss you, didn't say anything about fucking you" He had a point and I hated that.

"Enzo if that's what you called me up here for, you can forget it" I tried getting off his lap but his nails only dug into my hips sending pleasurable pain to my body.

Giving me the time to examine his tattooed filled body some starting at his collar bone to his strong arms. Grounded my hips on him, his eyes closed. Remembering he gave me the permission to touch him I used this opportunity. Tugging at his tie, his eyes opened. The amused smile on his lips asking for more, I grazed my lips on his.

"If you keep teasing me, I won't be afraid to break your only rule" he said meaning it. My nails running over his jaw, down to his chest I unbuttoned the black shirt only to reveal more tattoos with a small chest scar.

His arms spread on the arm rest he let gently place a kiss to the already healed scar. His lip tucked between his teeth, I used my thumb to pull it from his mouth.

"Cazzo.." he trailed off, the tent building underneath me I almost moaned at the size I was feeling. Hand around my neck he brought my head closer to him.

"Feel something you like tesoro?"

"Nothing I haven't felt before" I responded, the darkness in his eyes only growing along with tent in his pants. Constant knocking at the door made him groan. Luckily the heavy doors blocked words from the outside.

"Open up dickhead" someone said.

"This isn't over, wait for me down stairs hm?" Nodding I got up, opening the door a male similar features to Enzo leaned on the door with his legs crossed.

"Gorgeous" he greeted nicely.

"Violet wait for me downstairs" Enzo came up placing his hand on the smalls of my back. Feeling my body shudder a bit I excused myself from the intimidating men.

Helena waited at the end of the steps. "He'll just get rid of you like the rest."

"For someone who isn't dating him, you are really invested in his life" I sat at the bar, smiling at the nice bar tender who gave me a short glass of water.

"You'll never know Enzo the way I do."

"Give it up Helena, I'm his dancer now I suggest you come to terms with it" I haven't even came to terms with it yet. I was close to completing my first dance for him but it was interrupted, who knows what would have happened if it wasn't.

My phone dinged, over a ten thousand dollars sent to me by Enzo. Standing at the top of the steps along with the man from earlier he winked at me. Bringing the glass filled with a light liquid to his pink lips.

"He will never be yours" I scoffed.

"Do you really believe that?"

"You can't change my mind."

Finishing the last of the water I put down the glass, making my way up the stairs to Enzo he watched me with intriguing eyes.

"Violet" he said as my knee brushed up his thigh. The man behind him attention on me.

"You said our dance wasn't finished correct?" My thumb brushing his stubble.

"Well then let's finish it" I took his hand in mine leading him away from the stranger, once his door closed I felt a hard smack rain on my ass twice today. His hand around my neck from the back he pushed my ass against his front.

"I'm the one in charge, but I also miss your body falling apart on top of mine" he spun us around so no he was back on the couch with his legs open.

"First off" I got on my knees. "I don't fall apart, that's your job" I ran up my hands on his thighs, fixing his seating position he opened his legs wider for me.

Stopping my hands where he wanted them the most, watching me strongly. "Is that so?" jerking his hips up my hands found their spot over the growing tent.

Eyes dripping with intensity I sat on his thigh not fully on his lap. My knee lightly grazed his covered dick through his pants. While my hips rotated onto his thigh. Enzo gripped my hips quickening my pace. His head now on the chair rest, I brought his attention back to me.

"Eyes on me" the right amount of friction for us both, this time it was my eyes that closed. Fixing my self in the middle of his lap my fingers slipped into his hair, hands now on the side of his face. Lifting my hips before going down he cursed out in a different language. Holding my breast in my hands feeling my harden nipples, his tongue darted out licking his bottom lip.

Removing his tie, it tightened around my neck. "Cazzo" he said I turned around so now my back faced him. The tips of his fingers lightly touched down on my back. My knees still on either side of him. My back arched down giving him a few view of my ass. Both of his hands going down my back until the stopped on at the curve of my ass.

Pulling me up by his tie he raised my hips, trailing his hands up the inside of my thigh gently.

"No one is allowed to see you do that but me" I couldn't ignore the feeling from my throbbing core.

Taking my curls into his hand he pulled my head back. "Understand" he squeezed my thigh.

"I understand."

The curtains of his office hiding the mid night light, holding me up by his tie he threw open the curtains pressing my breast against the glass.

"You're body is to addicting to show off Violet" Facing towards him the coldness of the glass was nothing compared cool sensation of his silver ring on my neck.

His erection poking my thigh, my lip fell between my teeth. Hooking one of my legs over his thigh I felt it by my already wet pussy. "Is something the matter." he acted clueless.

Tracing the sharp line down his chiseled jaw, our lips an inch away from each other the smallest breeze traveling through the small space.

"This won't end well Enzo" Tension between us was thick, the teasing, the dominant man he was it wasn't good for me, the tattoos falling down to the tips of his fingers down to his chest.

Enzo Romano would bring me nothing but chaos.

"We're the authors of our own books tesoro, we choose how it ends, I know how I want mine to end."

"How so?"

"I want you against that window staring down at everybody while I fuck you until you can't walk" he stated bluntly, my thighs trying to clench themselves together only to be blocked from doing so by his thigh.

"I want you screaming my name while no one gets to hear the pretty sounds that falls from these lips" Daring me to take his finger into my mouth probably wasn't the best idea to do, but I did.

"I would love to see you on your knees for me."

Falling down into my knees, I was playing with fire messing with him. "Like this Enzo?" But who didn't enjoy playing with fire and getting burned a little.

"You'd look better with my gun in your mouth" devilishly smiling down at me, the front of his pants in my face. My eyes flickering up to him down to his bulge in his pants, my nose only barely touching it.

My hands laying on the floor, the crowd outside having zero clue what's going on right now.

"Would I?" he squatted down to me, the crystal blue look in his eyes imagining many ways of fucking into me with his gun in my mouth or on my body. That would be such a new experience for me, you could call it one of my deepest desires I would want fulfilled by a man like Enzo.

"Mr. Romano, we've got a problem" someone outside said. Enzo helped me up removing his tie from my neck.

My temperature still trying to calm down, inhaling and exhaling didn't work, trying to restrict myself from fanning my body.

The bouncer from earlier pointed downstairs to the loud screeching from outside. Valerie came out of the other room with Enzo's brother, her shirt missing holding his shirt to cover her body.

"What is it?"

"One of the dancers got into a fight." from the staircase Helena was being pulled away from one of the other dancers by her waist trying to what I think was claw her in the face out.

Enzo rushed downstairs coming up with her by her side, spitting words at her in Italian. She smiled at me like she won the lottery before returning to a fake act.

Without another word their voices disappear behind the door he locked.

Valerie pushed the man away from her coming over to me.

"I should get going" she nodded waving me goodbye then pecking my cheek.

Taking my trench coat from the room, I said goodbye to the man who made sure I exited the building safely.

Sitting in the uber I thought off looking out the window.

Enzo would be on my mind all night.

□

/ □□□□□□□ □□□□□□□□ ?

□ □ □ □

□ □

"□□□ you sure you'll be okay with her?" I fixed my mother's pillow behind her back. I recently got enough money to hire a home nurse for her, to take care of her when I'm at work.

"I assure you everything will be fine" Her nurse's name was Anne, her short cut red hair styled in a small ponytail in the back. Leaving her a bowl full of chopped up fruits along with sliced pancakes dining in syrup.

"I'll see you when I get home okay" my mother weakly held her hand up to me, kissing her cheek I shut the door to her room.

Locking the door of the apartment I bumped into someone. "Excuse me bella" he said.

Shaggy brown hair with small curls on top, he pounded his fist on Daniel's door. Daniel opened the door seeing me first ready to yell at me until he saw the stranger next to me his face turning into one of pure terror at the Italian man.

"Mariano crap.. what are you doing here" he cleaned off the small pizza crumbs on his shirt.

"He wants his money Danny, he hates waiting you know that" Mariano patted his cheek. Taking the knife from his pocket he placed the sharp blade in the middle of Daniel's chest.

"I haven't gotten it all" he glared at me.

"Get the money soon or I'll carve my name on your stomach got it" Daniel nodded furiously.

"Continue with your day" he said to me with a nice smile leaving.

Daniel once again grabbed my wrist, the smell of junk food and beer coming from his mouth.

"Get my money by tonight" he seethed slamming his door in my face.

A black car right outside the building with a kind gentleman outside. "Are you Violet?"

"Yes"

"Mr. Romano requested me as your driver for the time as his dancer" He was a bit short, but he seemed really friendly. Opening the door for me in the passenger side he jogged over to his side.

"Excuse my manners signora, I'm Garrett" I recognized him now, he was the man that always helped me walk to my uber when I went home.

It was also so dark a night we didn't even recognize each other in day light—he drove down the streets but the place we went wasn't the bar.

"Where are we going?"

"Mr. Romano requested you to meet him at this location" It was a cafe with a fancy opening on the outside—something told me this belonged with him also. Enzo only sent another check to me this morning with no message.

Helping me step out Garrett opened the door to the cafe, the smell of delicious pastries floated around the room. In the back of the cafe sat Enzo in a black turtle neck, the gold watch on his wrist. His black hair neatly sitting on his head. His arm on his lap, he had no idea the way the ladies in the cafe stared at him with the same thoughts running in their heads. If he was aware then he simply didn't care.

Laughing at something one of the guys said to him, he threw his head back in laughter. The view of his adam's apple had me stuck in place.

The woman at the desk eyeing me weirdly as I passed her to meet Enzo. The men sitting around him scanning my body along with Enzo, but his stare was the most distracting . When I sat down his arm went around my waist moving me towards his side more.

"Good morning beautiful" I recognized the voice being Mariano, he pressed a kiss to my hand. Enzo scrunched his eyebrows in confusion before the looked wiped away.

"Mariano" I said waiting for someone to explain to me why I was here and not at work.

Enzo snapped his fingers making them all stand up and scatter around the bakery.

My body sat still feeling his fingers run up my arm softly. "Why am I here Enzo?" he turned my chin to him.

"Fix your attitude, I don't take it well." The brunette woman placed two coffees down on the table.

"Tell me why I'm here Enzo" he closed the black shades around us. Tightly cupping my chin, his eyes darted down to my now split lips.

"I'm going to tell you one more time, watch how you speak to me Violet." the threatening manner in his voice only made it worse for him. I rolled my eyes, without getting the chance to register anything I was sat on his lap.

Keeping my face close to his, the mint of his breath fanning over my face, his hand creeping up my beige colored skirt. "I don't want to see you to roll those pretty eyes of yours unless I'm fucking into you." Trying to stop the feeling of my pussy wanting to grind down on his hardness, I suppressed the words that wanted to tell him to fuck me.

Keeping quiet, the lace material covering my core was pushed aside. "Look at you already so wet for me amor" running his finger up my wetness before placing his two digits into my mouth.

"Suck" doing as told his watched with hooded eyes.

"You're going to ride my fingers until you come" dragging his now salvia covered fingers down my chest to my pussy once more, my mouth gaped open when his fingers entered me.

My hands on his shoulders. "Enzo we're in public" the bare shadows of people walking back and forth ahead of us, oblivious to what was happening.

I was worried about the fact that we were in public and not that my boss's fingers were curling at my spot just right.

"Judging by the way you're moving with my fingers, I don't think you care" My dress bunching at my waist, kneading one of my breast in his large hands the feeling of his touch on my skin was delicate but it brought flames everywhere he touched.

"En-" he shut me up by sticking his fingers back into my mouth, sucking them as I moved down on his fingers, his thumb putting the right amount of pressure onto my swollen clit. Now staring at me with lust- filled eyes, his eyes solely concentrated on my lips.

"Come for me, and me only Violet" Curling his fingers he laid his tongue flat on my neck, his feather like lips knowing exactly what to do. Feeling my orgasm ready to spill through me I buried my head in the crook of his neck. Letting my moans go, a vibration sent directly to his skin.

Taking his fingers he placed them in his mouth sucking off his now coated fingers. It was the sexiest thing I've seen in my life. Enzo was the sexiest man I've ran into moving here, but he was also my boss.

"Delizioso" he said in a low voice. Fixing my underwear I fixed my hair back in it's low bun sitting next to him. Someone opening the curtain, Mariano took his seat again winking at me.

Enzo's hand stayed put on my knee protectively, it went high before I stopped him. The grin on his face disappeared when the next man and took a seat.

This man was older than the both of them, grey strands of his hair on his face. Expensive watch sitting on his wrist, he looked no more than sixty but young all at once.

"Ciao Ms.Violet" Was there someone here that didn't know my name?

"Please just call me Violet" I held my hand out, just like Mariano he kissed the back of my hand.

A secure hold on my thigh, I looked to see Enzo only throwing darts at the older man.

"Mauricio" The waitress came back with shaky hands giving Mauricio his cup of coffee.

Taking it to his lips his eyes still stayed on mine.

"If you don't mind me asking, how old are you?"

"I'm twenty two" he rose an eyebrow fixing the tie on his neck. A screeching car coming up in front of the cafe made all three men whip their heads towards the front of the glass door. Mariano smiled wickedly at whoever just got out of the car.

"Mariano do me a favor and take Violet next door, get her whatever she wants" Mariano groaned putting whatever was in his pocket away.

"Where are you going" I said to Enzo, his jaw was clenched still focusing on the outside door.

When he didn't answer I took Mariano's hand following him out the back, taking me into the jewelry store he played with the tooth pick in his mouth.

The cashier greeted us, her brown skin beautifully glowing in the light of the fancy store. Her curls full around her face, her lips covered in a little amount of gloss. Mariano looked like he had seen a goddess when she said hello to him again.

He only nodded at her, laughing at how his cheeks turned a light tint of pink, I continued to look at the nice bracelets.

Mariano never left my side just watching me unless his eyes traveled over to the lovely cashier.

"She's pretty isn't she?"

"Yes"-

"I mean no.. wait yes but she's more than just pretty" he walked with me threw the isle of gold necklaces.

"Then go ask for her number" he shook his head no.

"Why not I'm sure she think you're more than pretty also." he smiled standing in front of me.

"I'm probably not her type" As he said that Enzo walked in with his fist closed tightly at his side rushing past us. The gust of wind the flew past him as he walked behind the store to the back.

"Don't worry about him gorgeous, just in one of his moods" Mariano shrugged. Throwing his arm over me we left the store.

"Hungry" At the same time he said that my stomach rumbled as an answer.

Leading me threw the terrible crowded street, I stayed close to Mariano as people ignored me bumping into me.

One man harshly bumped into my shoulder calling me a bitch. Before he could walk off Mariano grabbed him by his collar, his fist connecting with the guys nose a loud crack rang in my ears.

"You respect her got it, now apologize" the man holding his nose stuttered out an apology to me before running off.

"You didn't have to do that." his arm still around me.

"I did and I wanted to"he held me close, Mariano was good looking. He carried a knife on his hip at all times, it had the letter M engraved on it.

Still walking he twisted it around his finger showing me tricks he learned. Landing it between his fingers, I asked to try before he laughed saying I would probably kill us both. He wasn't wrong.

We sat in the restaurant eating when Enzo barged in.

"Where the fuck were you two?" he said more to Mariano not even acknowledging my presence.

"She got hungry" he said calmly eating the bread.

"I've been calling you for the past two hours" he boomed, I don't think Mariano deserved to be yelled because my stomach.

"Why are you yelling at him, I was the one who got hungry and lost track of time" Enzo's head whipped to mine, the rage apparent in his eyes.

Was he really upset because I wanted to eat?

"I wasn't talking to you" He said loudly. Mariano check his phone seeing the miss calls from him.

Motioning his head at me, the guy named Andrew took my arm. Taking it back from him, Enzo stood up towering over me easily.

"Get in car Violet" I scoffed, he didn't get to come in here and ruin a fun moment because someone messed up his day. Whether he was my boss or not Enzo couldn't talk to me how he pleased.

Mariano stood up behind me holding my hand. "Gorgeous just wait for me in the car" the action only seemed to tick off Enzo more.

"Listen to him Violet" he grinned.

"Fuck you Enzo" I bumped his chest hearing his footsteps follow me out into the dark street.

Yanking my arm my back hit his hard chest. Spinning me around he pinned me to the car door.

"You don't listen do you, did earlier not teach you anything" leaning towards me, the hold on my neck only hardening.

"Do I need to put that mouth of yours to better use?" The metal of his rings on my burning skin, I should be pushing him off and cussing him out but my body and mouth betrayed me.

I hate to admit it but Enzo was sexy when he was angry.The turtle neck making him look even nicer today, I couldn't even concentrate on what was happening.

"You're not allowed to speak to me like Enzo" I crossed my arms.

"You piss me the fuck off Violet can't you fucking see that" Violet stop being a damn whore and focus, but I just couldn't the tattoos on his hand on my throat.

Dammit my thoughts was way to far from innocent right now. I was too busy thinking about angry car sex and not the fact my legs were freezing.

"How bad?" he tilted his head closing the space between us. The urge to pull his neck down and smash my lips onto his was growing stronger.

"How bad do I piss you off Enzo, tell me" My hands now on his belt. Standing in my heels giving me the ability to reach his ear.

I pressed a kiss below his ear. "Tell me how bad you want to fuck me against the car"

□

/ □'□ □□□□□□ □□ □□□□□ □□□□□□ □□□□□□□□ □□□ □□□ □□□□ .

□ □ □

□□□ □□□ didn't understand the way her voice affected me, she didn't get the things her words did to me. For someone who wouldn't let me kiss them, Violet sure liked to tease me with her lips. Her chest rising, her lips softly kissing my neck, the seductress was trying to get a reaction out of me.

"Get in the car Violet" feeling her smile on my skin her nails went down on the nape of my neck, her body fully pressed against mine.

"Make me Enzo" She definitely knew what she was doing, either she knew I was going to listen to her stupid rule about not kissing or she wanted to see how far I would go until I finally broke. I wanted to know who would break first, but if she kept getting me hard like this I would definitely crumble.

Getting ready to say something blaring sirens rung snapping her out of trance. I opened door quickly shutting it when she got in. "Enzo what's happening" she asked. Mariano walked out just in time to handle them.

"I'm taking her home" I told Mariano, getting in the car Violet went to talk but she didn't.

When the car came at the red light her view was on the glittering stars in the night sky. "What exactly is it that you do Enzo?" her hand resting on her chin, propped up on the console blocking me from taking her in this car.

"That's a question you don't want the answer too" looking at the address she typed in the gps. I knew exactly where she lived without even having to follow the directions.

"I can't work for you if you keep secrets from me."

"I don't know you well enough to tell you" her well manicured hand resting on my upper thigh.

Parking in front of the building I stepped out, the drunks on the street running away as they saw me.

Violet stepped out, she held my hand tightly. "Is something wrong?" she bit her lip nervously.

Using the pad of my thumb to remove her lip from her teeth. "Stop biting your lip, now tell me what's wrong."

"I forgot something, it's not important" I could tell she was lying but she was eager to get inside of her apartment.

"Would you like me to walk you up" I didn't trust this neighborhood at all.

"No it's okay, my mother is home" humming I held her chin up to look into her coffee colored eyes.

"Sleep well tesoro, I'll pick you up tomorrow" The want to kiss her full lips only built up more. Dammit she was so stubborn.

"The rule Enzo" she breathed, knowing she wanted it to I leaned in closer. "It's getting late" though her lips told me no— her body leaned forward. The exchange of champagne on her tongue clouding my nose.

I was Enzo Romano, I took what I wanted whenever without caring but fuck, something was holding me make from claiming her lips. The day I did take her lips to be mine, they would always and only be mine.

I wouldn't let Violet be my weakness, yes I was drawn towards her something about her smart mouth, her features gracefully given to her. Her fucking body was perfect. If I was to go farther with Violet than I wanted to it would be used against me.

Nothing good came from my lifestyle or my family's name, at a young age you never choose which path you wanted. It was given to you by your parents, some got the normal, bloodless happy ending, people like me got the hell of it.

The first time I watched blood drain from someone's body was when I was sixteen, sleep less nights along with the haunting nightmares, the feeling of my body starting to grow cold. I tried everything to stop those fears from returning, pills, sex, even just not sleeping. Nothing worked until I got used to it all, to the point watching someone take their last breath didn't bother me anymore.

Violet stood trying to watch the memories run in my eyes but my blue eyes only came up with pure blackness.

"I'll see you tomorrow" I let her walk into the building until I saw her figure disappear behind the second door.

The drive home long as it always was, opening the door the maids welcomed me as the always did dismissing them for the night I didn't want anyone near me tonight.

Taking the scotch from the cabinet I poured it in the glass throwing it back. Ignoring the bitter taste, I removed my shirt.

Helena walked down the steps, red lingerie clinging to her fit body. Her black hair tied up in a pony tail, strutting over to me her red heels sounded down on the floor.

Getting on her knees I pulled her ponytail back. "What are you doing here?"

"You look stressed, let me help" taking my dick out of my pants her red lips wrapped around my tip.

Helena seemed proud that I let her suck me, the whole time I imagined pulling Violet's curls while thrusting my dick down her throat, thinking about her brown eyes staring up at me instead of the green ones now tearing.

Fuck, the thought of Violet with my dick in her mouth along with tears spilling on her cheeks only made me harder.

Moving away from Helena she stood up asking what happened. Fixing myself I opened the door for her.

"Get out" she grabbed her robe walking over to me.

"B"- I shut the door in her face, removing my clothes I got into the shower.

My eyes closed thinking about Violet and her body, events from earlier of her ass out for me with her back arched, my hand found it's way to my dick.

I had to get her out of my mind.

□

"□□□□□□ please the money is in the apartment I'll go get it" I said trying to break free from his harsh grip, Daniel had a knife slash on his neck now covered in a white bandage.

"I'm sick of getting in trouble for you" his hand came across my face. The sting still lingering there, Anne and my mother were in the apartment safe. "Look what they did to me because of you, you stupid bitch."

"Daniel I have your money just let me go" I pleaded, Enzo would be here any minute and I didn't need him to see this or anyone. Daniel was screaming through the walls probably waking up the rest of the tenants but none of them spoke up about Daniel's abuse.

I had left over money from paying Anne to get my mother he medicine, enough saved up to pay this months rent but Daniel wasn't having it. The harsh gash on his neck stretching down to his chest.

"You pay me twice a fucking month now" he pushed me down to the floor. Hardly yanking my curls back his nasty smile came back. "You won't like what happens if you're late again." he shut his door. Knowing Daniel I knew what he meant, the thought only making me gag.

Rubbing my scalp I went up stairs into my bathroom fixing my self. The money on the table waiting for me to give it to him, I slid it under his door.

It had been over twenty minutes and Enzo still wasn't here, Garrett instead showed up with an apologetic look on his face.

"I'm here to pick you up instead, I got you a bagel sandwich just in case you waited out here past breakfast" thanking him I got into the black SUV.

Mariano was first to stand up from the booth, his signature tooth pick in his mouth. "Gorgeous" he engulfed me in a hug. Valerie soon came over doing the same with Enzo's brother making sure nobody looked at her.

"He's like my guard dog" she threw her arms around him, Damien rolled his eyes saying hello to me before they continued upstairs.

Mariano took me to the bar getting me a drink. "I took your advice and went back to get her number"he showed me the piece of paper with nice cursive writing on it.

"That's great" he smiled brightly. My attention went from Mariano to the back of the private booths. Helena swirling on the pole while Enzo sat and watched her, throwing money directly towards her.

So much for being his only dancer. Mariano followed my gaze before sighing. "Don't think to much of it."

Helena slid down the pole seeming so happy that Enzo was with her right now. i'm

"I don't like the look in your eyes" Mariano said next to me. To the side of the booth a man already focusing his grey eyes on my body, telling Mariano I'd be right back he told me this wasn't a good idea.

The contract states I would be the only dancer for Enzo, that no one else was allowed to touch him other than me. Too bad he already broke it that was his choice, closing off the booth with its red velvet belt I sat myself on his lap.

"Name?" I took my time to examine his face, definitely handsome, brown hair, a cut running along his cheek, the nicest hazel colored eyes I have ever seen.

"Nicholas" he said, finding my waist with his hands he waited for me to begin. My chest on his now my ass rotated on him, laying my head on his shoulder hearing the sound of his heart beat quicken.

Nicholas's thighs opened more trying to feel more of me on him, turning around Enzo caught my eye from across the room. The furious look on his face only made me smile at him, blowing a kiss at him. I arched my back down, doing the exact same move he said he was only allowed to see. Feeling Nicholas slip money continuously into the strap of the satin set on my body, my ass moved in the air for him.

My eyes on Enzo the whole time when I held my breast, his jaw ticked standing up. "Why is Enzo Romano staring at me like he wants a bullet between my eyes, you're not his girl or anything right?"

I knew Enzo was close enough to hear my next words that's why I said them. "I'll never be his."

"Is that so" I faced Enzo, the dark glint in his eyes seemed like he was going to prove me otherwise.

"Indeed, now if you excuse me Mr.Romano, I'm with a client" Tugging me up by my arm, I felt Nicholas's presence disappear behind us.

"I told you, I'm the only one you dance for" he held my waist.

"You also said that you'd pick me up this morning and that I was your only dancer, I guess both of those were lies weren't they." He smirked arrogantly.

"We're you jealous?"Closing the small gap that was amongst us he pinched my hip. "Did it upset you that she was the one entertaining me and not you?"

Taking his tie off I wrapped it around the back of his head pulling his face down to my own, my lips craving to finally taste his, by now the private area was shut now, the curtains covered us. Seeing the sexual attraction we felt for each other, I knew Enzo could feel it too.

"I would never be jealous over someone like her, I could do better anyways" he rose a brow.

"Is that so?"

"Show me then" Planting himself on the chair, I climbed on top of him.The curtains being thrown open Helena walked in throwing me a deadly look.

Getting off of Enzo he stood up keeping my body next to his. "What is it?"

"You left so soon" she completely ignore me next to him. "I thought maybe someone was being a bother."

"I see you've two have a lot to chat up on, I'll go entertain the others, wouldn't want to keep them waiting" I was going to pay for that later but testing his patience was fun. About to exit the curtains his voice cause me to halt.

"Violet, wait for me in my office."

/ □ □□□□□□□ □□□□□□□□□ □□ □□□□□ □□□ □ □□□ □□ □□□□□□ □□□ □□□ □□□□

♥

□□□□□

□□□

□

□□□□□□□ for Enzo was not going to become a new thing, when he finally opened the door his white shirt was cuffed up to his forearms expressing his many tattoos. His black hair laying over his face before he pushed it back, he removed his tie calling me over. Something was going to happen and I was going to let it.

His thumb pressed down on my tongue, looking up into his blue eyes that drowned me in the best and worst ways, Enzo was a man of many secrets, secrets that would kill him in the end. He was cocky but he had many reasons to. My wrist were being tied, secured with one last tug.

"You would look so good bent over my desk" Nothing came good from when he smirked. Folding his small handkerchief into a neat roll he pulled down my bottom lip, stuffing it in my mouth his lips found their way to my neck.

The electricity I felt when he touched me returned, the door was locked thankfully though I don't think Enzo would stopped if someone knocked. His tongue brushed over my sweet spot on purpose, holding my wrist behind my back Enzo led me to his chair, back on his lap his lips never left my neck.

"No one is allowed to see this perfect body of yours but me, got it" Knowing I couldn't respond his lips curled into a smile on my neck.

My words coming about muffled by the handkerchief in my mouth a hard weapon placed on my covered clit. Looking down at his hand, the gun tickled my skin yet brought pleasure to aching nub. Shutting my eyes I thought about it, I couldn't have slow developing feelings for someone who cared only about him self.

"Look at me bambina" I was biting on the material so hard my jaw started to hurt, I wasn't going to allow my self to fall for him, I couldn't look into his sapphire's and find the thing I've been longing for.

To be more than just a body.

"Look at me Violet" Taking out the handkerchief from my mouth. "I need your lips."

"Enzo the rule"- our chest closing the small space between us, I was lost once again in the perfectly trimmed stubble on his jaw, his eyelashes that hit his high cheekbones, the dimples I never get to see unless he smiles when he truly means it.

The rule was an excuse, I couldn't careless about it. The desire look in his eyes told me the same, this was the time someone knocked on the door, but the knock never came.

The breeze of the room circulating around us along with his pleasing aroma. Fuck me.

Tilting my head down, his tongue darted out to lick his wet lips. "Cazzo, ti voglio"he breathlessly said.

"Enzo" My next words would break my own rule but who cares the contract had already been broken when I signed it, how did I expect to work for a man like Enzo Romano with out feeling the sexual desire for him. "Kiss me" without another word his lips claimed mine, deeply yet passionately. They were just as soft as I thought they would be.

His lies, lust, and eventful life would soon become mine, untying my wrist my hands wasted no time to find the black strands the drove me insane when they weren't styled they way they always were.

His tongue thrusting into mine allowing me to taste the delicious scotch that left its prints in his mouth, at this point my panties were soaked over a kiss. I felt like a virgin who just got her first kiss or just had sex on the way my body was loosing itself.

Missing the feeling of them Enzo bit down on my lip enough to draw blood, his blue eyes looking into my own with hunger, pain was what he wanted to bring to my body but he brought the complete opposite.

Swiping the small blood that trickled down my lip away with his warm tongue he moved to my neck. "Enzo" I moaned in his ear, feeling him underneath me growing harder by the second he pulled away.

"For your safety tesoro, I'd sit still" The tone in his voice telling me he wouldn't have a problem throwing me over his desk and fucking me senseless.

I would love that.

"What are you thinking about?" The glint in his eyes returned devilishly, I had forgotten about his gun resting on the inside of my thigh. The sting of my panties ripping I glared at him. "I'll buy you so much more."

The base of it finding my needy nub. "Oh fuck" his tattooed hand coming around to my neck, keeping my lips next to his, Enzo watched my hips try to find my release on the unloaded weapon.

"My name is the only one that gets to fall from these gorgeous lips of yours understand" Frantically nodding my head. Squeezing the sides a bit more I let out an erotic moan. "You like this don't you?"

"Riding my gun until you come again for me" Holding his shoulders, I took his hand placing his fingers in my mouth, bringing them down to where I needed them the most he grinned devilishly.

"You want my fingers, is that what you want."

"You have to say it, I can't understand you when you're whimpering into my shoulder." I hated him so much but my need to come was stronger, still circulating my waist on his gun I needed more.

Tossing his gun to the side of the couch my aching clit was begging for him so was I. "I need your fingers, please I need them so bad" I stuck my bottom lip out into a pout seeing his eyes fall into a pool of greed.

Thrusting one finger into me my body frenzied, pulling down the skimpy dazzled bra, my brown nipples feeling warmth being taken into his mouth.

The blissful feeling of his thumb still pressuring my clit along with his fingers finding my g spot before he focused on that one spot only. "Enzo I'm going to cum" I cried out, dammit I found myself wanting way more than just his fingers, if I could only just ride his fingers I wouldn't complain but the member constantly teasing me through his pants was calling out for me.

"Go on then, make a mess on daddy's fingers" One final curl had my body falling from its euphoric state. If the walls weren't sound proof I'd probably be heard by everyone down stairs and underneath us.

Tasting his lips again he fixed my outfit, my panties still laying on the floor ripped he handed me his suit jacket. "I'll pay for it don't worry" biting my lip he used his thumb to remove it from it's hold.

The sound of Damien's voice came from behind the door. I sat besides Enzo on the couch, covering my body -when he stood up to open the door. Damien's eyes fell on me before returning to Enzo.

"He's here" Enzo must have understood who he was talking about because he nodded before closing the door.

Bending down to me on the couch I once again fell back into the blue pools of his eyes. "I need you to go home"

"Garrett will be outside for you hm?"

"What's wrong?" I stood up putting on his jacket on. "Questions I don't want the answers to got it, but tell me one day okay." he looked uneasy and didn't reply.

My phone dinged with a message from Anne.

"What is it?" Enzo snapped me out of my daze, Daniel is banging at my door upsetting my mother.

"Nothing, I need to get going." I opened the door only to be gently pulled back into his body. Holding my waist he traced his finger down my stomach kissing along my neck.

"You forgot to kiss me goodbye bambina" Enterally smiling I spun around bringing his lips to mine.

"I really need to get going."

"Take Mariano with you, and be ready at 8" I rose my eyebrow smiling.

"Is this your way of asking me on a date Mr.Romano" he backed me into the door, bent down now close to my face.

"I'm not asking you Violet, I'm telling you" His dominant voice made me weak in the knees. The boldness in my body flew directly out the window.

"I-I'll be ready."

□

□□□ hours it had been since I sent Mariano to take Violet home safely, since those two hours we closed down the building. Henry Del Rosa sat with Helena next to him, Helena was his daughter, the only reason I put up with her and not killed her was because she was the closest connection I had to ending his life.

"You said this is all of it" I held the white bag filled with cocaine, handing the bag to Cruz he examined it bumping my shoulder.

"Would I lie to a man like you Romano?" Henry said with his Spanish accent, "I wouldn't dream of it" I didn't trust Henry, I didn't trust anyone but Henry was a sneaky asshole. Selling his daughter off to different mafia's just for money. When he tried selling Helena to me just so I wouldn't kill him, I knew what type of man he was from that same day.

Helena gasped when I shot at her father directly above his head making him shake in his seat. Standing in front of him I let my gun rest on the side of his face. "Pensi che questo sia uno scherzo?"

"I don't do not favor your life Henry" I roughly held his face, my finger on the trigger that would send the bullet directly into his skull.

"I would give me the rest or I'll let your daughter watch her father bleed dry, you wouldn't want that would you" he shook his head quickly tossing the rest of the bags on the table.

"Smart man" Alejandro said from the side collecting the rest of the drugs.

Seeing the sweat starting to trickle from his forehead Henry closed his eyes tightly. "Please it'll never happen again" Using his daughter like some type of shield, Henry Del Rosa was a pathetic man.

Getting in my car I drove home, the lights off I turned them on again. Removing my clothes I got into the shower, rinsing the expensive soap from my hair I let the curls fall on my forehead. The towel around my waist.

I watched the wind blow the black drapes into my bedroom, finally putting on my watch my door bell rung. Spraying the last of the cologne on my body, I opened it to see Violet.

Fucking hell.

Her silky legs not being covered by the brown dress, it showed off the rounds of her cleavage not leaving much to my imagination, her fingers nervously intertwined with each other, the brown dress only hitting her thighs, it was buttoned up stopping where the crack in her breast began.

Her crumbed neatly up in a bun with some strands coming loose, her bottom lip tucked in her teeth as she peered up at me through her long eyelashes, her brown eyes examining my outfit.

"I said I'd pick you up."

"I know it's just that, Mariano said you'd much more appreciate if I came to you instead." she pointed to his car pulling out the driveway.

Letting her enter her eyes widen, she was focusing on the interior of the house while my eyes wondered off to her round ass. It moved with every fucking step she took.

Coming up behind her, her body froze seeing her gulp down on nothing. "Y-you're house is amazing"she stuttered out. Her dress leaving her back exposed I ran my knuckles down her bare skin.

Her hair smelled like coconut with a mix of honey, her lips covered in light gloss, I pulled her bottom lip out of the hold from her teeth. "Bite your lip one more time, I won't be able to control the thoughts I'm having." her breathe hitched.

The door flew opened making me wrap my arm around Violet protectively, taking my gun out I aimed at the man standing at the door.

I recognized him from earlier, he was Henry's second in hand. He pointed the gun at me then at Violet making her jumped holding onto my arm for dear life.

Quickly shooting him in his arm he dropped the gun, that's when everything in my body erupted when the bullet landed at her foot. When he fell to the floor I lifted him up by his shirt, my gun repeatedly finding his skull. He begged for me to stop which only gave me more fuel to continue. The inaudible gasp from behind me faded away when I stuck my gun directly at his chest.

Standing above him I looked directly into his eyes barely being able to stay opened before the sound of the bullet rang along throughout the house.

□

/ □□□□□□ □□□□□□ □□□□□□□ □ □□□□ □□□ □□□ □□

□ □ □ □ □

□□□□

□ "□□□□"- Violet said standing behind me, the only view I gave her was my back towards her, my gun directly aiming at the man on the ground choking on his own blood. I was waiting for her to say that this isn't me so I could yell at her and tell her that this was who I was. To show her what I meant, why everyone coward away from me when I took her home the other night. She only kept quiet watching the scene unfold in front of her pure brown eyes.

"Merde" I said to myself not wanting to turn around so she would judge me, I didn't care if she would walk out of this door and choose to never see me again. The scarlet blood poured out onto the floor, I tensed when a hand was placed on my back.

"You need to leave." I said coldly, I needed to clean this mess up and figure what the fuck he was doing here, then I needed to find out how he found my address.

"Get the fuck out Violet" I directly yelled at her, she played with the ends of her dress still watching everything in front of her.

"You need to tell me." I walked towards her, her small figure backing up towards the table in the dining room.

"I don't have to tell you anything" her chest rose and fell all together, the fact that she could look me in my eyes after watching just what happened. "If you don't get out I won't be responsible for my next action."

"What are you going to do kill me too" I towered over her, her neck having to crane up to look at me, I held her chin with the gun.

"I could if I wanted to." Already missing the sweet taste of her lips I placed the gun on the table behind her. "Don't you understand, how bad I am for you" it's like she was ignoring everything she witnessed like she's already seen it once before.

"My mother is sick Enzo, my life is already falling apart around me, you aren't the worst thing I've come across" she admitted, the emotions flowing through her eyes when mentioning her mother. "Even if you did kill me right now" she stood taller on her heels holding me close by my black collar.

"You'd be doing me a favor asshole" she smashed her lips onto my own, her gloss now on my lips I lifted her by her thighs feeling them enclosing around my waist. Removing her hair from its neat bun I tangled my fingers in her soft curls. Pulling her head back I let my tongue work it's self on her neck, smelling her coconut body wash along with the nice smelling body lotion that made her skin soft.

Her breast in my face asking for my attention, I unbuttoned the dress with my teeth before returning my lips to her beautiful brown skin, her lower half rubbing down on mine. Her body was fucking addicting, she was addicting.

Her silky skin on mine, her fingers in my hair trying to take some control, I sank my teeth into her bottom lip taking all of the dominance back. The power hungry kiss made me want more, more of her.

"I hate how bad I want you."

"Hate me all you want Enzo, hate my body even more" The seductress started her own attacks on my neck, leaving her teeth mark on my neck I groaned grasping her ass. My cock twitched in my pants, I wanted her against this kitchen, on this table, in the shower. I needed to see her body wrapped around my sheets.

"You piss me off." I set her down, her nail lightly scratched my jaw. Both of us breathing heavily.

"You piss me off more." As she said that Alejandro walked through the door with Rowan.

"I see you have a two special guest" Alejandro said looking at the body on the floor, Violet placed her hair back in its bun.

"Kevin" he held his hand out for her, the kind person she was she smiled at him shaking it.

"Alejandro" Alejandro wasn't a Romano but he was still very close the the family, the deep scar on his eyebrow went down to his cheek. Alejandro came with his own demons, just like Mariano he had his own things with knives.

"Violet Bianchi" they continued to clean up the mess, Violet waited for me to say something.

"I can't tell you everything."

"Then what can you tell me?" her hand placed my shoulder, moving it off of me her lips fell into its natural pout.

"I can't tell you anything, I need you to leave."

"We aren't doing this again Enzo" she rolled her eyes.

"We aren't doing anything, get out."

"If I leave Enzo, the contract is over with, I will no longer be your dancer anymore. I will dance freely for who ever I choose to dance for." Poking my tongue at my cheek her eyes were serious.

"Is that what you want?"

"Will you tell me what the hell it is that you actually do" Looking at the time it was way past midnight, I had other things to worry about more importantly I had to find Henry Del Rosa.

In order to do that I would have to speak to Helena.

Not responding she grabbed her purse walking towards the door, seeing her hips sway she turned to me. "Then you don't get to throw one of your tantrums when I give someone else the dances you just gave away" she shut the door.

□

□□□□□□□ my mother the food she refused to eat, she finally calmed down after tonight. Her sharp in takes of breaths worsened, she wouldn't eat, she didn't want to drink water it was breaking my heart to see her like this.

"I love you Vio" she always told me she loves me, after my father disappeared on us her sickness intensified. I sent Anne home for the night because I wanted to be alone with my mother watching her favorite shows, her once healthy curls now only damaged and loose, her body to weak to even lift up her hand.

I was saving money for her treatment but I was barely even close, now with not dancing for Enzo, lower money came in. Was it wrong of me to want to know what his job actually was? It clearly wasn't owning a bar and a strip club because he killed the man in front of me with no remorse, he's had to done it before. I wasn't scared of him because it wasn't my first time seeing someone brutally murdered.

It happened a lot in the neighborhood my mother and I used to live in, I cried myself to sleep at times thinking about it. I saw my father constantly tell my mother that he loved her, her brown eyes that used to smile along with her, now only broke more at the thought of him.

"I love you more" I gave her, her last bite of the food before leaving her to sleep.

I wish I could do more for her, give her the luxury house and lifestyle she deserved. I had taken another job at a bakery from across the street of the Enzo's club, the more money I could bring in the faster it would to pay off the treatment to finally get her into her surgery.

A familiar grunting voice knocked at my door, looking through the small peep hole it was Mariano but he didn't look well. Opening it for him, he stubbled in holding his side.

"Mariano what happened" I struggled to help him sit on the couch. Lifting up his shirt the bullet hole opened allowing his blood to slowly come out. In his hand was the bullet.

"I-I took it out my self but, shit this hurts gorgeous" Even on the verge of possibly bleeding out he still complimented me. Rushing into my bathroom to take the first aid kit I turned on the light to see the wound better.

"This is going to hurt" he looked at me in confusion, I took care of my mother half of our lives, I could manage to fix a shot wound.

Cleaning around the areas I threw the bloody towel into the trash, helping him remove his shirt he groaned in pain.

Making sure the bleeding stopped before I put the burning liquid on his body he clenched his fist. "Would you believe it.. if I said this is my first time getting shot" he joked.

Finishing the last of the stitches I gave him a white bandage to help tame the bleeding, two Advil pills thrown back in his mouth he took the water bottle trying to stand up. "If you stand up right now you'll rip your stitches."

"Aw gorgeous I'm flattered, do you care about me" he held a hand over his heart.

"No, I'd rather you not bleed out on my carpet while my mother is asleep."

"Fair enough" we laughed lowly when he winced at the pain. "What's got you so down" he sat up.

"Nothing important, how'd you get shot?" he sighed seeing his phone dead.

"Can't tell you" I stood up throwing his shirt at him.

"Why are all of you so secretive, it's like you all work for the FBI." He mumbled something under his breath.

"I heard about your talk with Enzo" I sat down next to him. "He's not an easy man to get to open up, I've known him forever and there's shit he doesn't even tell me" he took another sip of his water.

"You can sleep here tonight, you can't even get up properly" I handed him a blanket.

"I'll wash your shirt" I didn't want to talk about Enzo, I didn't want to think, or hear his name.

Which my mind betrayed me on because he was in my dreams.

"Goodnight gorgeous" I heard Mariano say from downstairs.

□

/ ♥

□ □ □ □

□□□ □□□□ and I avoided each other the like the plague, it had been a week since I last saw him, he wasn't at the bar, his stairway up to his private room was completely shut off. I recently been dancing for a man named Julian Rossi, he was a touchy man. I made sure he knew he wasn't allowed to touch.

He paid well, he definitely dressed wealthy. I brought his drink over to him. Damien had also taken his own leave of absence, Valerie seemed unbothered by it dancing for the crowd of single men. I helped the bartender with the busy place, the bakery across from me definitely helped getting more money.

Sitting on Julian's lap, five well-dressed men walked through the doors, Enzo being one of them. His grey shirt a bit unbuttoned, his tattoos prolonging on his skin. Helena went up to him pecking his cheek with her red stained lips, walking up with her to his office.

I needed to speak to him about ending our contract permanently, I hadn't noticed Julian saying something in another language behind me. He was French, his accent thick, he had a little trouble with my name but I found it cute.

"Will you excuse me?" he asked politely, letting him get up Valerie came over to me.

"I seriously need to get drunk, and I mean fall on your face in the street drunk."

"Are you free tonight, if so meet me back here at ten it's when all the fun happens" she nudged my shoulder.

"I'll be here" The girl from the jewelry store came in looking around. Getting up she smiled when she saw me.

"Is Mariano here?" if it wasn't for her deep brown skin she would be red right now the way she bit her lip at his name.

"I haven't seen him all day" Mariano left when woke up leaving a small note that he had something to take care of.

Her face fell a bit before she nodded. "If you do see him can you tell me to call me, I'm Angel" she said.

"Violet" Angel was beautiful, her hair was short and curly, her brown skin was unbelievably clear, she had dark brown eyes but they were light at the same time.

"I should get back to work" she gave me a small smile before leaving. One of the bartenders called for me to take the drinks upstairs into the private room.

"Do it for me peaches, I've got business to take care of" Freddy said handing me the tray with drinks and a box holding cigars.

"Only because I love you" Freddy kissed my cheek thanking me, the tall guard with large muscles that could choke me to death denied me from continuing up the stairs.

"I need to see Mr.Romano please" he kept looking forward not acknowledging me.

Realizing that I wasn't going to leave unless he let me through he opened the velvet rope. As always the hall was dark, knocking on the black door the smell of smoke fuming from inside.

Helena opened it with a victorious smile, letting me enter the men turned their heads to me. On the table laid bags of cocaine along with other drugs, guns on each of their laps. In the middle of all of them sat the devil himself.

Enzo's gold chain sitting on his collar bones, the snake tattoo running up his forearm to his bicep. Helena ran back to his side to her place on his lap, he watched me with his intense scan of my body, the look able to make anyone fall to their knees for him. His black hair in its natural state, the sky light blue in his eyes peering at my chest when I bent down to place the tray in front of all of them.

"Cazzo.." one of the guy's said behind me, the short black skirt showing off my freshly shaven legs. Some of them giving me dirty looks as I took in the weapons around me, the drugs on the table along with the stack of money around Enzo.

I definitely wasn't supposed to see this.

"Everybody out" Enzo announced, the all left even Helena who rolled her eyes at me. I was left standing in front of him, his seating position how it always was, legs opened, hand resting on his jaw.

"You've been dancing for Julian Rossi" he lit the cigar bringing it to his lips, my lips suddenly felt dry.

The puff of smoke free in the air, he sat up straighter running a hand over his stubble. "That's none of your business." he grinned standing up, coming over to me the remaining scent of the smoke mixed in with his cologne.

"It is my business when you work for me." Enzo must have forgotten about what happened two weeks ago, just up and leaving then coming back like I was still his personal dancer.

"About the contract, I would like it to be terminated" The walls seemed to be closing around us, the air choking me all together. "I'm opening a new one with a new client, he wants a more private session" I kept my head up seeing his nose flare.

"That wouldn't be a problem with you will it sir?" My mother always told me my mouth would get me into trouble, I believed her I purposely said things to piss Enzo off more.

"Not a problem at all tesoro, but I'm afraid Julian won't be able to sign that contract." I furrowed my eyebrows.

"And why is that Mr.Romano?" his hand snaked around my waist possessively. My body flushing against his, his piercing blue eyes jumping in jealousy at the thought of me on Julian.

"I won't hesitate to put a bullet in both of his eyes for looking at you the way I'm supposed to" I scoffed, shivering a bit when his hand grasped my ass tightly.

"It's to late for that don't you think, you ruined any and every chance with me. At least he tells the truth" the centimeter between our lips telling one of us to give into the others teasing ways.

Moving away from he returned to his seat. "Come then, let me tell you what it is exactly that I do." Part of me felt like this was a trap but he was serious. "You need to trust me tesoro."

"I know about you Enzo, you cannot ask or wish for my trust when you are a stranger to me."

"My father's name is August Romano, Italian mobster until he turned fifty two, my side of the family is known for transporting drugs, weapons, different deaths all over the city."

"That would mean your family is apart"-

"We aren't apart of it darling, we are the Italian mafia, the main family if you prefer, Violet my family isn't safe nor trustworthy. Things no one should have there lives exposed to."

"Wait if you're part of the mafia do you do human trafficking?" I kept my stance but the chilling idea of something so revolting made me want to run out that door now and leave everything.

"No tesoro, my family may be monsters along with their dark demons but we don't do anything other than what I've told you." he brought the drink up to his mouth taking a large gulp.

"My father's mafia is now mine, which makes me the Don, those men you saw earlier all work for me." I kissed the world's infamous mobster, I let him make me come along his fingers. The same fingers he uses to pull the trigger to end a person's life.

"So killing people is apart of your every day life?" I couldn't judge him because I was the one who wanted to know, though it was too much to process. The drugs, the body two men helped him clean up. When I turned on the news this morning it was covered up as a suicide.

"Only when needed." he stated bluntly. "Look at me" I kept my eyes down to my sparkling black heels refusing to meet his gaze. "I need you to understand now that you know, you cannot tell anyone"

He gently raised my head. "If you don't keep this to yourself Violet" he pushed a curl out his way so he could lean close to my ear, placing a small kiss on my earlobe. "You will be killed, along with whoever you tell."

"That's if I don't kill you myself." My breathing almost came to a full stop, it was a lot to take in but he was cancelling out any of those thoughts with his hands roaming along my body.

"You couldn't kill me Enzo." My subconscious was telling me to shut up before he actually proves me wrong. He rose his eyebrow, his pink tongue licking his bottom lip.

"Why is that amore?"

"Simply because, you enjoy my presence so much." I felt his hardness on my thigh, I skimmed my hand to it making him curse something in Italian.

"Now if you excuse me, I have a client to attend to, wouldn't want to keep him waiting." I proceeded to the door opening it, being around all the drugs started to rush back to me.

"See you tonight Mr.Romano."

"□□ visto molto capo" Preston says next to me, the blonde woman in front of me tied up, her mascara running down her face filled with tears. She was wondering off and ended up in the warehouse during a sell. I yanked her blonde ponytail back seeing her makeup smeared all over her face. (She's seen to much boss)

"Who sent you" she shook her head, there was no fucking way she just ended up all the way over here from getting lost. Pressing my knife deeper to her neck, she only sobbed more annoying me.

"I-I promise I just got lost" Mariano flicked his knife from it's hold. Her body trembled with fear. "Please if I tell you, he'll kill my son." she finally said.

"Quindi inizia a parlare principessa" Damien came in with Valerie on her side. Damien wasted no time showing her his gun. (Then start talking princess)

"I can't my son"-

"Either you start talking or you won't have to worry about him killing your son" he squatted down to her height. Valerie turned away taking a gulp of her water.

"Please he's only two, he has him right now" her crying only grew louder irritating me.

Taking her by her neck she squirmed at my touch. "I don't care for his or your life, now tell me who sent you here."

"I-I think his name was Leo" she finally let out when my hand almost took her last breathe. Letting her go she gasped for air.

"Deal with this" I said to Alejandro, Mariano following me out the warehouse the midnight sky along with it's illuminate stars as we got into the car driving back to the club.

The loud music booming from the back to the front, the dancers in their own private booths, it was crowded filled with drunks being tossed out.

"Her mother isn't just sick, it's like she's dying" Mariano said out of no where. "That night I spent at her house, she was up in the middle of the night crying in her mother's room." He never told me he was at Violet's house he only told me he got shot during a wrong drug trade.

We took a seat in our area along with two other girls stripping their bodies, one trying to hand me a drink I shot her a stare then she backed away.

Valerie soon entered with Violet. Merde.

Violet wore a tight black dress, her brown skin enlightening in the different colored lights of the bar, her lips lined with light gloss that always tasted like caramel. Her silky toned legs I wanted around my waist, her thighs I needed to frame my face while I tasted her delicious pussy that was always so wet for me.

Julian called her over, she smiled at him leading Valerie over there sitting on his lap. His hands on her curvy waist. I wanted to cut off his hands and send it to his family for touching what was mine.

She whispered something his ear before taking his hand, leading him to the middle the music slowed. Moving her body at the rhythm of the music, she kept her hips swaying back on him, his hands touching on her body.

"It looks could kill, he'd be dead right now" Mariano said besides me. When her eyes lifted to meet mine, the deviance in her coffee colored iris's led to the corner of her lips puckering at me, blowing me a kiss she turned her body to him.

Allowing his hands to grabbed her ass, the smoothness of the back of her thighs looking directly at me. Julian didn't know what to do next, I could tell from here it was bothering Violet.

She needed control, someone to keep up with her stubbornness, she wanted someone to put her in her place when she spoke the way she did to rile them up. I left for the last two weeks trying to find out the true identity who Leo was, earlier wasn't my first time hearing his name. He had been around since my father was in charge of everything, he was a con man, and a lying thief.

Making my way over to her when Julian went outside to finish a phone call I moved my hand to her hip. Bending down to her ear, her sweet scent of coconut was enough to get me high. Her hand reached around to my head leaving it's place in her neck, no words were spoken only lustful touches were given.

I needed Violet so bad, I needed her plumped lips around my dick, I needed to feel her clenching around me. Dammit I wanted her so fucking bad, this wasn't good for any of us but I don't think she cared. A little side of me knew she wasn't fully sure about me being in the mafia or how to take it. I wouldn't put her in danger, neither would I let her get to attached to me.

"You're a confusing man Enzo Romano" she said with her eyes directly on the dancer in front of her.

Spinning her around the desire in our eyes met. "What ever do you mean tesoro?"

"One day, you act as if you hate me with all your heart, the next you become some jealous beast" The lights dimming lower, I could see her eyes trying to figure me out. "Why can't you just play nice?"

Trailing my fingers down her exposed back her body fell to my touch, her body was so responsive to me even if she didn't like it.

"There's nothing nice about me Violet" her eyes flickering between my eyes to my lips not knowing which to look at. She brought her own closer to mine trying to close the small space separating them.

"That's where you're wrong Enzo" her new acrylics traveling down to my hair down to my jaw.

"I'm the nice in your shitty life"

□

/ □□□ □□ □□ □□□□ □□□□ □□□□ □□ □□□ ?

□ □ □

□ □□□□□□ □□□□□□□ □□□□□ ⚠

□

□□ was only a few minutes before Enzo was leading us out the bar to his car, the lavish vehicle with it's black leather seats, he drove down the streets in a quick hurry, not caring about the red lights or the beeping cars. A new place he entered with the tall black gates matching the black interior. Two large looking men bowed their heads to us.

Opening the door he slammed it closed with me pressed against it. Capturing my lips with his own he lifted my leg up with his arm. His fingers tangling in my kinky curls, I moaned into his mouth when his tongue found mine dancing together in the hungry pace that was his kiss. Unbuttoning his shirt I got to see his perfectly sculpted body along with all his tattoos I wanted to scratch my nails down.

His belt buckle was next to be removed leaving him in his boxer briefs, looking down at his cock begging for my attention I bit my lip.

Leading me upstairs to his bedroom, it had a balcony allowing the moonlight to flow freely throughout his huge room, sliding my dress down my body. His eyes darkened staring at my black lace, it was crotch less along with nothing hiding my erect nipples.

Standing much taller than me his black curls fell over his face, his heavy breath basked in mint. His nails digging into my hips the pleasure of the pain making me whimper. Claiming my nipples with his mouth, he toyed with the other in his hand, lips never leaving my neck.

"This is the part where you tell me to stop" he said against my skin.

"Violet tell me to stop and I will" the feeling of his soft lips igniting flames throughout my body, my lower half becoming warmer every second I felt the delicacy of his touch.

"Enzo" I couldn't bring myself to say stop simply because I didn't want him to. I wanted his hands roaming over my body, while he held my neck thrusting into me. The erection I felt on my thigh made my mind wonder off. Pinching my him since moaned lowly when he hooked my legs around his waist.

"That's not telling me to stop amore" removing my shirt over my head his lips patched onto my swollen nipples, my hands shot in the softness that was his black hair.

"Tell me what you want."

"Fuck me Enzo" The smug look on his face told me he was going to make me wait a bit longer for what we both yearned for.

Tracing my bottom lip with his finger, the need for him only growing. "You want to be my good girl don't you?"

I nodded but he wanted more, taking a handful of my ass in his hands. "Say it tesoro"

"I want to be your good girl Enzo" he went back to the bed until he was propped up on his elbows.

His open legs telling me to stand between them, situating myself on my knees the cold floor hurting me but I didn't mind.

"Go on then, show me how good you can be for me." Removing his hard cock from his boxers, I could barely wrap my hand around it. He watched me with hunger eyes seeing my reaction to his length.

Wrapping my lips around his tip he groaned biting his lip, making sure I kept my eyes on him he moved my curls out of his way. Taking him down my throat he held my head down lifting his hips more. My gag reflex relaxed allowing him to fuck my throat.

Enzo finally let my head up making me gasp for air, the trail of saliva on my lips being collected with his thumb pressing it to my lips. "Keep going, you're doing so well amore."

Using my hand to stroke the part I couldn't fit in my mouth I let my tongue swirl around his veiny shaft, seeing him throw his head back I continued to twist my hand around him.

"Play with your clit for me" listening to him I rubbed small circles around my clit as I took him deeper into my mouth. Standing in front of me now, he pushed the tip to my lips before controlling the speed of my head. Leaving my tongue out whenever he slid out of my mouth he cursed up into the air.

Using my finger to enter my tight hole Enzo praised me in Italian. "Cazzo, I'm going to cum" he held my hair in a ponytail not leaving me any room to relax my throat he thrusted his hips hitting the back of my throat.

Feeling white strings of his cum on my tongue, I opened my mouth so he could see me swallow the salty release. Stroking my cheek sweetly with his thumb he lifted me up.

"You're a slut you know that?"

"You're my slut though, my good fucking slut" placing me flat on my back he opened my legs for him to hold my thighs close to his face. Enzo pressed a kiss to my not- so flat stomach, then up to the valley of my breast finally to my lips.

Blowing a cool breathe over my already wet pussy he laid his tongue flat on my core. "Keep your arms up" I listened to him when he starting to lick all my juices lightly collecting my clit into his mouth, sucking for dear life I moaned out load. The guards down stairs probably heard me but I couldn't help it.

Enzo spelled his name along my skin, sucking on my thighs Enzo used his teeth to mark the inside of my thighs. "This pussy belongs to me only" only being able to moan out his name more he gave me a satisfied hum sending vibrations along my body.

His tongue fucking into me while his thumb pleased my swollen nub. I couldn't help my hands play with my nipples, he slapped the inside of my thigh still looking up at me. Moving my hands back up I felt the euphoric feeling rip through my body.

"Enzo.. oh fuck" Not stopping Enzo was going to make me cum again. "It's too much" I tired moving away from him on how good he was making my sensitive clit feel. He kept my thighs locked in place giving me no room to run.

"No you can take one more tesoro, you can do it for me can't you" Harshly holding onto his black curls I came again on his tongue. He stood up, licking his lips clean closing his eyes at my taste Enzo kissed my lips letting me savor the taste of my sensation.

Taking the condom from the table on the side he rolled it down his length. Teasing me at my entrance I yelped out for him to fuck me already.

"Tell me how badly you want me to fuck you Violet, how badly you want me to fuck this tight hole of yours."

"Please Enzo, I need you to fuck me" I begged but he clicked his tongue.

"You can do better than that" He entered his tip in before pulling out.

Whining I pulled his neck down to me. "If I knew your were going to wait this long to fuck me, I would have went home with Julian" I didn't get to prepare when he slammed inside of me making me cry out.

Holding my neck down his tattooed arm looking so good keeping me down. Hitting my spot without trying, Enzo's body on top of mine was such a sight, snapping his hips into me his absurd words spilling out of his mouth in his language.

"Tell me tesoro, could he fuck you like this?" Not being able to talk, he squeezed my neck harder, my eyes shot opened when his thumb pressed down on my clit.

"No.. he couldn't" he leaned down into my ear still holding my neck, Enzo kept his fast thrust along with enjoyable feeling. My toes curled around his waists

"That's right, because Violet" he pressed a kiss to my neck. "You.Ar e.My.Fuck.Toy" he said with every jolt. Speeding up my hands found the headboard of the bed when he turned us around. Bounding my hands behind my back Enzo kissed my shoulder to my neck, feeling his breath fan over my neck along with my hair sticking to my forehead. I had never felt this good before, I wasn't a virgin that's for sure but my past ex's were nothing compared to Enzo.

Enzo was marking me all over, inside and out with everything he had, his cock only making my walls wrap around him tighter, he moaned my name in the air. Hearing his Italian accent along with my name was the sexiest thing I've heard, his hand around my throat now Enzo's hand connected with my ass.

"I'm going to cum Enzo, please don't stop" His arm around my stomach making sure I don't try and move away from him.

"Come for me Violet, come on my dick" My walls clamping down on him my body fell slump only being held up by my neck. I came undone, he still didn't stop. "I know you come on more time, come on be good for me" My eyes were tearing, the tears hitting my hot cheeks. His hand snaking around to my clit, my fingers pulling on his locks he moaned at the pain liking it. Another orgasm close Enzo sped up chasing his own.

My mouth fell opened feeling his dick twitch inside of me, his finger nails breaking the skin in my hips. "Fuck" he said before we came together, slowing down he pulled out of me. My breathing still labored.

It was going to be hell to get up, luckily Enzo held me bridal style but he was quiet. His bathroom was way to nice, the black tiled shower and floors along with the walls and the marble sink. There was pure silence when he placed me in the warm water leaving the bathroom.

A towel on the sink, his body wash smelled good like he did, when I wrapped the towel around my body and entered the room he was gone.

So was my dress along with my lace set, a grey shirt with basketball shorts waited for me on the bed. My thighs ached climbing into the silk white sheets. The only thing on my mind was that I just had sex with Enzo Romano, a mobster.

That left as soon as he got what he wanted from me.

□

/ □□□□□□□ □□□□□□□□ ?

□ □ □ □ □ □

□□

□ □□□□□□□□ shine of the sun from outside woke me up from my sleep, my dress freshly washed being placed down by a woman in a short maid like outfit, along with a tray off breakfast left next to it all.

"Ms.Violet, Mr.Romano has his personal driver ready for you when you're ready to leave" she said closing my door, my lower body felt sore all over. Removing Enzo's shirt from my body I put it in his closet. I did feel a bit hurt that he fucked me and left, it made me feel like that's all he's just wanted was to fuck me and act as if I didn't exist.

The fresh toothbrush with the berry scented lotion and spray waiting for me in the shower I quickly got ready. Enzo's new house was better than his last, the decor matched who he was as a person.

I hadn't time for breakfast so I took the croissant making a small breakfast sand which. Opening the door Mariano waited for me in his black shades covering his eyes.

"Gorgeous" he hugged me pressing a kiss to my temple. "How'd you sleep?"

Other than feeling like I was used for my body. "Great." He eyed my sandwich carefully.

Holding it up to him he took a bite. "You're a lifesaver you know that" I laughed as we continued down the stairs, more familiar faces including Alejandro, Rowan, and Damien sat in the kitchen.

"Buongiorno" They said together, giving them a small wave back Mariano stayed by my side until we got into the car. The driver already greeting us I buckled my seat belt.

"Do you know where Enzo went?" Mariano had been fixing his glasses since we got into the traffic.

"Where he always goes" he replied like I knew the wherever that was. Shaking Enzo from my thoughts the car parked in front of my house, Mariano led me inside. Daniel forcefully grabbing my wrist— he didn't see Mariano behind me.

"You bitch"- he let go of my hand when Mariano appeared behind me with a sadistic smile.

His eyes burned in rage seeing the now red hand mark on my wrist. "Mariano I didn't know she was with you" Daniel coward back into the wall.

"Gorgeous here, she's a really good friend of mine Danny" His knife came into my view, remembering what Enzo said about him being in the mafia it all came together now.

Mariano noticed my expression turning to me. "Go take care of your mother okay gorgeous" his smile turned sweet for me. Sparing Daniel one last glance he looked scared for his life.

Closing my door I heard Daniel begging for Mariano to stop until the sounds died out through the hallway.

Anne was in the kitchen making my mother lunch, I remembered to pay her last night from what Julian gave me. "She's taken her pills from last night, so far her breathing has become stable" I smiled thanking her going up stairs to my mother.

Opening the door her blue sheeted bed was completely emptied along with her bathroom.

"Anne" I ran down stairs making her drop the plate. "Where the fuck is my mother?" Just at the time my phone rang with the call from her hospital.

My heart exhilarating picking up the call. "Is this Violet Bianchi" the doctor spoke.

"Y-Yes" I was already grabbing my key's out the door looking for Mariano or the car but it was no where to be found, Daniel's apartment door busted.

"You're mother has been picked up for her treatment" I texted Garrett asking him to drive me, when he finally arrived here I got in running my hands through my curls with confusion flooding my mind.

"What do you mean for her treatment?" I had maybe thirty other payments to complete before she was sent into surgery.

"We can discuss the rest when you arrive Ms.Bianchi" Garrett seemed to understand when I pointed the way to the hospital— the doctor hung up and my heart was beating through my ears.

Questions flooding my mind— every possibility was crowded my brain.

When Garrett arrived I ran out of the car through the glass hospital windows stopping at the main desk. "Meredith Bianchi please" I said to the woman with the nice afro, she typed quickly before giving me the room number of my mother.

Room 205. I opened it seeing my mother laughing along with the doctor holding her hand. I threw my arms around her gently around, my eyes watering she hugged me back.

"Tell me what's going on someone please" I said in her curly hair.

"Well Ms.Bianchi, your mother will go under surgery in the next two days" I faced her doctor.

"But how.. I haven't finished the payments?"

She smiled showing me her clip board. The donation sent of all her payments complete even the after surgery fees paid off completely.

"Who.. who did this?" my mother held my hand, her own tears forming in her pale brown eyes.

"I believe his name was Enzo Romano"

□

□□□□□□'□ blood puddled at my feet after Mariano brought him here telling me what he did to Violet— Daniel confessed his abuse to her for years, when he told me all that he's done, thought about doing to her my blood boiled —I didn't give him the chance to plead for his life when I shot him between his eyes.

Washing my body under my shower— my eyes closed, visions of my younger self running along the halls crowded my mind, my mother pointing out my dimples I inherited from her. Dimples that do not show anymore because I don't have a reason to show them anymore after her.

The soft knock at my door only pissed me off even more, leaving the towel around my body I didn't bother drying myself off.

I was met with my favorite pair of honey brown eyes, an over sized sweater covering her sexy body of hers. Scanning my freshly showered body her eyes fell dark. She didn't speak before she wrapped her arms around my neck pulling my lips down hers, bringing her inside I shut the door lifting her up by the back of her soft thighs.

Biting down on my lip, the seductress this time found my tongue with her own allowing me to taste more of the caramel on her lips. Gripping her curvy waist I sat on the bed with her on top of me.

Pulling away she kept her hand on my cheek along with her forehead resting with my own.

"Thank you so much" she said leaving a small peck on my lips.

"You don't have to thank me tesoro, I know how it feels to see your mother sick without being able to do anything about it" her eyes saddened for me.

"I thought.. I thought you didn't like our night together that's why you left me" I knew that was coming, I didn't leave Violet because all I wanted was her body, I just didn't know how or if she wanted me with her when she woke up.

She played with her fingers looking down at my torso, holding her chin up I could see the insecurities of her past running through her eyes.

Flipping her so she was on her back she bit her lip watching my wet curls fall over my forehead. "I did more than like last night tesoro, I couldn't get you" I pressed a kiss to her neck. "Or your addicting body" then one to her nose.

"Out of my mind" I left heated kisses on her skin, her nails lightly scratching down my back.

"Enzo" she breathed softly, my name from her lips sounded so perfect. Something that was supposed to mean death and destruction in my world came out peaceful from her.

"Tell me what you want" I thought about Violet all day, even when she was alone in the car with Mariano even though he made it clear he was her close friend I still didn't like the idea of her bonding with someone that wasn't me.

Fuck what was she doing to me.

"I want you Enzo, please give me what I want" I took her bottom lip out from her teeth.

"For you tesoro, I'd give you the world" I said before claiming her lips again, her hands removing my towel.

"Eager are we?"

"You're a tease, it's not my fault" she laughed, the sound alone making me smile before covering it up with a cough she frowned.

Placing her small hand on my cheek, "You have a beautiful smile Enzo" she ran her thumb over my dimple. "Why don't you smile?"

"I don't have a reason too."

"What if.. what if I was your reason." she averted her eyes to the moonlight out the window.

"I'm just saying because I like your smile a lot.. so if I was your reason, I'd be able to see it more."

"Don't go shy on me now Violet, look at me." she slowly turned her head to me.

"Mr.Romano, she's arrived" the maid said from outside the door before I could tell her something. Violet sat up while I fixed my towel.

"Stay here, I'll be right back" she looked down at my body then back up to me, grabbing a shirt I threw it over my body before putting on my sweats feeling her watching me.

I looked at her through the mirror. "See something you like tesoro?" she turned away.

Leaving the door I went down the steps seeing Reyna sit on the chair talking to Alejandro.

Coming up to me she ruffled with my hair as she always did. "Mi manchi Enzo." (I miss you)

Reyna was a family friend, from her short black hair to her green eyes, her arms filled with tattoos.

"Reyna, you don't come by unless there's trouble, what is it?" smiling as she does when she knows I'm right.

"Ale says you have a special someone waiting for you upstairs, go to her we'll handle it."

Trusting Reyna I went up stairs to my tesoro, Violet sat on the bed on her knees, her thighs parted a bit allowing me to see what was waiting for me in her champagne colored lingerie. Now in front of her I lifted her jaw, smoothing my fingers down the lines on her back, her body shivering at my touch.

Removing my hard from my sweats, she slowly stroked me. Peaking up at me through her eyelashes she kept her eyes on me the whole time. "Fuck..just like that." Sliding her bra down it fell to the bed, using her tongue to take me deeper down her throat.

She pouted when I pulled out of her mouth, putting my thumb flat on her tongue she sucked hard. Laying her on her back I kissed her calf slowly.

"Tell me about your day mi amore" her eyes threatening to closed stopped when I smacked the inside of her thigh.

"I almost killed my mother's home nurse when I couldn't find her in her room" she kept her irises solely on me, trailing the kisses closer to where she wanted me the most.

"Mhm, keep going."

"Well I- fuck.. I.. Enzo please don't tease me" she said as my fingers parted her glistening lips. Seeing how wet she was for me I groaned, moving her closer to my me—I placed her legs on my shoulders.

"Tell me more" Violet huffed noticing I wouldn't give her what she craved unless she kept speaking. When she stuttered out about

Daniel missing, I kept my lips devouring her, her voice died out being replaced with her pants for me to go faster.

Her nails tugging on my hair, my eyes closed at the pleasurable pain, "Enzo... that feel good" I hummed while she raised her hips up, watching Violet fall apart was the sexiest thing ever, her body, her voice, the fucking sounds she made.

Fuck.

"Feel good for me tesoro" that's exactly what she did, she was beginning to loose herself she hadn't even told me to stop after she came twice, I kept going because Violet was a drug, one that I got hooked on, I wanted to get high off Violet, off her scent, her lips, her body.

I wanted to be intoxicated in her, in the good and bad ways.

I wanted to bring bliss to her body, sign my name permanently between her soft thighs, kiss my way into her mind so I was the person she thought about when she touched herself. I wanted my name to be the only one she remembered, I wanted to ruin the seductress in every way possible just to fix her all together.

Tears streaming from her eyes but I went on, biting down on her clit another release erupted on my tongue, cleaning her up with my mouth I went for one more until she couldn't take it anymore. At this point Violet's body was overstimulated, her eyes still closed trying to get her breathing together.

When she finally opened her eyes, I reached my hand out for her neck. Cupping her sensitive pussy she whimpered. "Mine, say it."

"Yours"

□

/ □□□□□□□ □□□□□□□□

* please ignore the name Rowan for now, Adora & Reid have a son named Rowan who is still a child & not apart of the mafia, I would go back and edit but it would remove the current comments *

□ □ □ □ □ □

□□□

□

□□□□□□□□□ I was sitting on Enzo's lap in his private room while he spoke about business with the other men in the room, the room smelled of the cigar's in their mouth blowing out the smoke. It had been a week since everything. I hadn't heard or seen from Daniel, my payments to him only to be returned the next day. It was like he had disappeared off the face of the earth.

Suspicious raised in my body but it was blinded when Enzo placed his hand in the middle of my thighs, I started helping Freddy with bartending so I had to wear the short black skirt along with the white tight button up that held my breast well.

"Questa è lei?" one asked to Enzo making him smile as he nodded landing small peck on my neck. (Is this her?)

"Mia regina" he responded, I sat awkwardly looking around like I didn't know they were speaking about me. When they left they left different types of guns on the table in front of us.

Enzo picked one up unloading it and reloading it before putting it in his waist band, giving me the view of his sharp v line. I would be lying if I said this wasn't turning me on right now.

His black shirt was short sleeved so I could see his strong forearms along with his tattoos. "I should probably go help down stairs" I went to open the door, pure usual Enzo closed it standing behind me.

"Stay with me a bit longer" his voice alone made my panties dampen, his arm snaking around my waist.

"I still have a job to keep Enzo."

"I want to ruin you Violet" he slowly unbuttoned my shirt, cupping my breast I let my head lay on his shoulder.

"Ruin me then Enzo."

"I don't think you're ready for that tesoro, when I say ruin. I mean in every way possible, every position." he held my ass back on his erection letting me feel what it was exactly I do to him. "I want to write thunderstorms on your skin, then let you draw your image on my own"

Facing him I let my lips only slightly touch his own. "Write them Enzo" my nails grazing his jaw.

His hands firmly holding my waist, we stared at each other not being able to choose whether to look at our eyes or lips, Enzo made his decision when my legs enclosed around his waist. His lips fiercely attaching my neck, biting down on the skin Enzo marked me as his, leaning my head to the side to give him better access, Enzo moved us to his desk. The papers flying on the floor he sat me on the table.

Lifting his head from my neck, I laid my own marks on his light tanned skin, the red mark now darkening— Enzo's hands went up my skirt his own nails digging into my skin.

Not caring about his shirt I took it off throwing it behind us, his perfectly carved abs along with the letters written in cursive inked in his skin. Enzo pressed him thumb on my clit though my panties feeling my wetness caused by him.

There was days we didn't need to speak to each other, we knew exactly what we wanted and needed.

The burning passion between our lips meeting along with his hands running all over my body studying each curve of me. Enzo knew my body, I knew his. Not being able to keep our hands off of each other, we became each other's weaknesses.

"Mine" he said once again on my lips.

I held him close, keeping my legs around his torso. "Yours" my shirt was next to thrown across the room, I moaned in his mouth when he bit my lip hard, his tongue tasting mine, he had the taste of vodka along with strawberries from this mornings breakfast.

Keeping a tight hold on his hair, I let my teeth sink into his pink lips. "Mine"

"All yours tesoro"

Even if I didn't want to admit it, my body completely submitted to Enzo. The stares we got this morning from people in my neighborhood when he took me home, the all looked at me like I was walking around with the devil himself.

Holding my head to the side Enzo kissed down my neck to my chest, my head thrown back when my nipples were met with his mouth closing around them, giving the other one attention he pushed my thong aside inserting two finger into me.

"Come on my fingers tesoro" My heels dangling off his shoulder as he kept his fingers thrusting into my tight hole, his other two digits into my mouth.

"What are you Violet?" he asked removing his fingers from my mouth.

"Your good little slut" he smirked in satisfaction removing his belt, Enzo's was rock solid for me pushing his tip into my entrance. When he finally pushed into me, I came once more.

Turning me over my hands on the desk he held me up by my hair. My mouth opened spilling all the moans he likes to hear, lifting my leg up on the desk I couldn't believe how deep he was inside of me. Looking for something to hold on to, he simulated my clit all together making me clench around him.

"Fuck, you're so tight" Enzo made me come at his words, our bodies meant for each other.

His right hand squeezing my nipple, my moans loudly erupting from my mouth, the tinted windows along with the sound proof walls blocking any one from hearing or seeing us.

"Enzo.. fuck" My skirt was still bunched up on my waist and my black heels still on my feet, my thong snapped against my skin. My eyes rolling to the back of my head feeling my legs trembling.

Kissing on my shoulder Enzo kept his arms around me to hold me up, hearing his own pleasure coming out of his mouth it only brought me closer.

"Come for me Violet" my hand holding his arm when my orgasm ripped through making me cry out his name one final time before I felt him spill inside of me.

Enzo spun me around connecting our lips together hard, my nails on the back of his neck clawing down his back along with the other marks I left last night.

"I don't think you understand how badly I fucking need you" he grunted. Getting on my knees I looked up at him through my lashes batting them.

Enzo watched with intense eyes when I took him in his mouth moaning around him, his own release mixed with mine still on his tip. Holding my hair up he roughly shoved himself down my throat.

Tears starting to build on my eyes, they fell on my cheeks, holding me down until the tip of my nose touched his pelvis.

Wiping the tear away from my cheek he bobbed my head for me. "You're so pretty when you cry tesoro" closing my eyes when the strings of warmness slid down my throat.

Enzo stood me up holding my neck. "I'll pick you up at ten" it wasn't ever a question when he talked about taking me on a date.

It's not like I was going to say no.

"I have plans" I messed with him fixing my clothes.

"Is that so?" he grinned down fixing his watch, then turning his head over to me with a sinister smile. Enzo made it clear to Julian and I that I was supposed to dance for him and him only.

I've gotten dirty looks from most of the dancers including Helena, Valerie told me not to worry about them because they treated her the same way with Damien.

Enzo ran his fingers through his disheveled hair trying to fix it then coming over to me. "Tell me what these plans are" his crystal blue eyes knowing obviously knowing that I'm lying.

"None of your business Mr.Romano, you have guest awaiting you outside" I moved away from him opening the door letting the well dressed men inside.

"Good afternoon" I said to all them, a finally wink to Enzo before I shut the door.

Mariano sat with his jaw clenched, when I looked over Angel was speaking to another guy.

"Mariano you can't ignore her then get jealous when she speak to someone else" he rolled his eyes puffing the smoke into the air.

"I'm not ignoring her gorgeous, it's just fuck.. how am I supposed to even talk to her." he ran his hands down his leg before standing up going to her.

The man backed away seeing Mariano towering over him, his hand on her waist. She turned happily into his arms hugging him.

Smiling at them I made my way over to the booth containing more suited men waiting for a dancer looking at the empty pole. Memories of my first night here seeing some of the same men I danced for that night including Enzo.

"Don't even think about it tesoro" Enzo said from behind me, licking my lips I leaned back more into his chest.

"I wasn't" I let his hands coming around my torso, Enzo's left hand went up my skirt feeling my warm center.

"I just haven't been on a pole since I became your dancer" he took my hand to a room I haven't seen before, inside the room was red but dark dimmed low lights, a silver pole in the center.

Shutting the door Enzo removed my shirt, seeing that I left my bra purposely in his office he wrapped his hand around my throat. "Fuck the date, come to my house" I smirked taking his lip between my teeth.

"You're taking me on the date Mr.Romano, then maybe I'll go home with you tonight."

"If you're a good boy for me" this made him take a hand full of my ass in both hands making me gasp.

"Then I'll be on my best behavior" pushing Enzo back on the couch he smirked. I bent down giving him the view of my ass, sliding down my skirt I heard him groan.

Leaving me only in my thong I climbed on his lap.

Enzo watched me with hooded eyes as I pinched my nipples the way he would. "You're going to watch me cum on my fingers" he tried to touch my waist when I slapped his hand away.

Holding his chin I pressed a light kiss to his lips. "No touching" Using my fingers I placed them in his mouth feeling his warm tongue touch the pads of them. Dragging them down my body I encircled my clit with them, slowly starting to shut my eyes I felt Enzo growing underneath me.

My fingers entering making me moan his name, I rolled my hips on my fingers letting them to curl. Imagining what Enzo would do, if they were his own fingers it only made me wetter. Enzo watched my lips fall open saying his name as he tried to get some friction on his raging hard.

Finally coming on my hands he placed my fingers in his mouth sucking off my juices before humming around them closing his eyes.

"You're going to kill me one day."

□

□ was finishing getting ready when Enzo sent me a text that he was here, taking my keys I walked over to his car. Enzo was dressed in a navy blue shirt that was a soft material, long sleeved covering his many tattoos along with the gold watch on his wrist. His hair slicked back neatly. Feasting his eyes over my body I'm guessing he likes my dress.

It was a dark red dress, the v cut on my breast showing the curves of them. It clung to my body perfectly, walking into his arms he captured my lips, when he pulled away I wiped the lipstick on his lips off with my thumb.

My curls now in braids cascading down to my ass, Enzo opened the door allowing me to step in. No driver this time, he got inside keeping one hand on the steering wheel and the other on my thigh.

His thumb soothing my skin sending comforting feelings throughout my body, peeking over at him Enzo looked good when he was driving, his tattooed hands driving smoothly throughout the night.

Enzo held my hand helping me out of the car, his black jacket in his hand. The view of this place was beautiful, the tall buildings, the gleaming lights on all of the buildings.

Our fingers intwined in one another Enzo pointed out different buildings he's been in before, the nice Italian restaurant waiting for us he opened the door for me to enter.

The male waiter checking me out before leading us to our seats, the chairs were on either side of the table but Enzo pulled mine closer over to his.

"Can I get you something to drink ma'am?" the waiter looked no older than twenty one.

Enzo decided on white wine before I could answer, annoyingly tapping his finger on the table.

The waiter fumbled with his pen as I looked up to him with a small smile, Enzo's hand still on my knee warning me with his strong gaze.

"I-Is there um something else you'd like ma'am" the boy stuttered out looking at my chest ready to spill from my dress.

"A new waiter" Enzo mumbled under his breath.

"No that'll be all.. Henry" He blushed when I read his name tag quickly coughing and walking off.

"You're cute when your jealous" I said to Enzo who was sending daggers at the waiter who was walking to the back of the restaurant before he held my chin.

"I don't get jealous tesoro, and I'm not cute" I rolled my eyes at his lie. Enzo soon stood up excusing himself as his phone rang.

Let's test his theory shall we.

Henry came back with our drinks ready to take our food orders. Henry's cheeks still flushed red as he stared at my lips. I went into a deep chat with Henry when Enzo returned, his face already morphed into one of irritation it only worsened when he saw my hand on Henry's bicep.

Enzo soon came over standing behind Henry making him nervous again. "Leave" he said sternly, Henry shyly waved at me before running off.

I twisted the pasta around the fork before bringing it to my lips, Enzo sat ready to leave. "We're going"

"I'm hungry" I pouted at him, Enzo pressed my bottom lip down.

"Violet, be a good girl and let's go to the car" Enzo asked another waiter to box our food for us.

Stepping outside, the wind hit my shoulders. Enzo put his coat around me, it was warm and smelled like him. Waiting for the man to bring his car around, I pointed to the largest building that had the view over the city.

Enzo drove us leading me up all the way. The dumbest idea I had because I was terribly scared of heights. "If you let go of me Enzo, I'll kill you"

He chuckled keeping me safe, his arms around me with his head on my shoulder. The view was breathtaking along with the breeze fanning over my face, the chairs and the lights around allowing me to take everything in.

"I wouldn't dream of letting you go Violet" I held on to the cold railing pointing up at one of the stars.

Enzo spun me around pulling me to him, my heart jumping looking into his captivating blue eyes.

"I need you to be mine Violet."

"More than just my dancer, more than just what we are now" he held my manicured hand, soothing a braid out of my face, Enzo leaned into my lips.

"Are you asking me to be your girlfriend Enzo?" I teased with him a little bit. My arm going around his neck.

"Usually I wouldn't ask, but I need you to know that this won't be easy, my life, being apart of my mafia."

"In that case I want every part of it" I moved my hand up to his jaw.

"Every part of you."

□

/ □□ □□□ 1□ □□□□□ □□□□□ □□ <3

□ □ □ □ □ □ □ □

□ □□□□□ was my mother's surgery, I was holding her hand as they prepped her. To my surprise Mariano walked in with flowers for her.

Kissing her cheek my mother smiled. "Are you the gentleman my daughter won't shut up about?"that's when Enzo entered along with a whole truck load of flowers for her.

"I think that would be him actually" Mariano said.

My mother seemed in joy but skeptical of Enzo all together, he placed the flowers around the room allowing the berry aroma to float around. He stood still by the door with a worried look before she spoke.

"I want to have a moment with him please" she pointed to the door. I kissed her cheek taking Mariano out with me mouthing "don't scare him off" to her.

"I would love to stay gorgeous, but Angel and I have date" he quickly hugged me before jogging out the hospital before I could respond.

Enzo soon came out with a smile on his face, his dimples showing as he walked towards me. I couldn't even speak when he crashed his lips on mine, hands traveling up my hips grasping my ass in his hands, allowing his tongue to find mine I pulled away.

The nurses around us looking with curious faces, when they saw Enzo some of them went away the rest gawked at him.

"What was that for?" I wondered what my mother had told him because Enzo was smiling from ear to ear.

Still holding my ass in his hands, Enzo kept his head in the crook of my neck laying sweet kisses. "Come to my place tonight" his voice deep and husky.

"I can't my mother's surgery, I want to stay when she wakes up" the doctors around us whispered to each other. Some bashing him for being seen with someone like me.

"I'll bring you back tomorrow, she said it's fine anyways" He cupped my face in his hands ignoring all the stares we got. That's what I liked about Enzo, When he looked at me it was only me, no one else in room mattered.

"Please tesoro" Enzo might not have believed me that he was cute but he is.

"Is she really with him?" One nurse said.

"He's too good looking for her" the other responded.

I took his hand leaving out the hospital not being able to hear the shit that was being said. On the side walk Enzo must have sense my frustration because he pulled me to the side making my back hit the brick wall.

"Look at me" I continued to look at the cars passing around the street. "I'm not going to tell you again Violet, look at me" I finally looked up to him.

Enzo brought my chin closer to him, the gold chain on his neck staring at me. "Go around the back and get into the car" the side of his eye moved to the street. When I tried to look he only blocked my vision.

"Enzo, what's wrong?"

"Violet, listen to me and do as I say" I moved but he pulled me back pecking my lips once more, disappearing around the corner, Xavier opened the door to the dark SUV.

"Peaches, don't worry he'll be fine" I got in the car, Enzo didn't even seemed disturbed like he knew what was coming. When Xavier opened the gates to Enzo's home letting me in first.

Valerie came up to me engulfing me into a hug. "Does this happen a lot?" I asked as we sat on the couch.

"It gets worse" she said sighing, turning on the television Daniel's portrait showed at the top.

The reporter pronounced Daniel dead for over a week. He was killed from a fatal bullet in his skull but before that he was tortured for over six hours along with stab wounds along his body.

"Bastard deserved worst" Valerie said besides me.

"Did you know him too?" she faced me.

"He sexually abused me one night, it took everything out of me to keep Damien from ending his life, but there is no denying Damien helped with this" She said calmly. Valerie had been with Damien for a long time, so she was used to this. I wasn't sure how long it would take me to come to terms with his life style but I was willing to try.

I soon went inside Enzo's room to take a shower, rinsing the soap from my body, I felt his burning gaze on my body every inch to be exact. I turned so the water hit my back, not leaving he only watch the soap surrounding my chest.

The water raining down to my feet I heard his clothes being removed. Keeping my eyes down on the water draining down, Enzo closed my legs around him. The heavy breathing coming from both of us.

"I need you to get ready for tonight." My voice got cut off as he slid himself into me.

"W-What for?" I let my head rest of the glass behind me. Enzo started slow strokes still not being enough for me to calm my noises.

"We have something important to attend to tonight" He groaned in my ear feeling my tighten around him.

"Faster Enzo please" he kissed my shoulder quickening his pace making me call out his name in his ears, Enzo placed me on my feet turning me around. My hardened nipples pressed on the steamy glass, holding my curls in his hand Enzo kept a strong grip on my hip whispering his thoughts in my ear.

Enzo explained how he wanted to use me as his fuck toy tonight if I behaved myself. I couldn't even think or process his words because of how much he was filling me up, Enzo turned me around keeping my on his waist thrusting into me harder.

His hand around my neck the water only glistening down his perfect body. His dark wet curls in my face, he still kept his chain on his neck. Creating dark marks on his skin Enzo cursed loudly.

My walls pulsating around him. "Hold it" I whined in his neck feeling myself growing closer.

"Enzo..please I can't" I uttered on his lips.

"Such a greedy little whore, fine then cum" with the last words falling from his mouth I came undone.

□

Valerie dressed me in a champagne colored dress swam down to my legs, leaving my curls into a neat bun she did my make up. I admired my body as I put on my dress when Enzo walked in.

His black suit with the matching gold handkerchief in his side pocket, he was fixing the cuffs when he looked at me through the mirror. His eyes darkening seeing my exposed back and how good my back side looked.

"Enzo" he hummed in response. "Can you help zip up the dress please" I said. He came over to me, the chilling feeling of his ring grazing my skin. Finally zipping up the rest he dragged his knuckles from the front of my chest down to the valley that rested between them.

The eye contact in the mirror was growing to be to much when he pulled me flushed against him from behind.

"You are beautiful tesoro" Enzo held a gold necklace in his hands placing it around my neck. It matched the one he wore around his.

"Thank you, you don't look so bad yourself" he deeply laughed, his chest vibrating on my back.

"Mr. Romano, we're ready for you two" the maid said from outside.

"Ready" I nodded taking his hand. The comforting feeling returned any time I was around him.

Enzo and I got into his car, his hand over my thigh as he drove up to the elegant building. Before we got out Enzo turned my chin to him.

"You stay by my side all night, don't speak to anyone not even the wives. If I'm not around you, stay closed to Mariano or Damien" he was dead pan serious.

"Understand."

"Yes Enzo" he kissed my jaw.

"Good girl" I held his hand tightly but he ran his thumb over my hand to comfort me.

When the doors opened it revealed over thousands of different people, all extremely dangerous men with scared women to there sides. Someone announced Enzo's arrival, Mariano took my hand as Enzo told he'd be right back. Valerie and Damien sat on one end laughing in each other's ear's. She was so happy with him.

Marino placed a drink in front of me. "How's your mother?" he said drinking his own.

"She's still in surgery she should be out in five hours" I was praying from the bottom of my heart that everything was going to go right.

The doctor texted me constantly on her updates, so far everything was going well.

Around us were older men, they looked around eighty or sixty. Younger women next to them, one of the old men eyed me before winking at me making me mentally gag.

The doors opened again, the announcer saying a women's name by Rebecca Saint.

Rebecca had long blonde hair curled to perfection, her green eyes running along the room. Her dress blood red, she had a fit body from what I could tell.

Her heels matching the room, she smiled when her eyes landed on Enzo but he was already looking at me. Enzo brought the drink to his lips smirking over at me. His blue eyes still scanning my body with dirty thoughts in his head.

Mariano took my hand as every one around us started to dance. Enzo came over pulling me directly to him. "Tesoro"

Enzo's hand around my waist leaving sensual kisses to my neck not caring around any one. The table in the far back watched us like hawks, many of them watched me only. They resembled him, Enzo moved my attention to him.

"Relax, no one can touch you tesoro. Not when you're here with me" he said before spinning me out, drawing me back into his arms he held my leg up. Dipping me lowly every one looked at us.

Enzo was setting fires around me, blowing them out not letting anyone or anything touch me. My hand still on his cheek, Enzo just stared to my eyes.

"Enzo" I said moved my eyes down to his lips. Enzo slowly brought me up lingering his eyes to my own gloss colored lips.

"Enzo, your father wants to meet her" anger flashed in both of his eyes when Xavier came over, Xavier was new. His dark brown skin with his short faded hair, he was around my age.

Enzo fixed his tie, holding my hand tightly when the man approached us.

His hair still black, the same soulless blue eyes as Enzo, the shadow of a dimple on his cheek.

"It's finally nice to meet you Violet."

"What do you want August" Enzo said through gritted teeth.

"I want to meet the woman that has my son wrapped around his finger that he won't even come visit me." he kept his eyes on me making me avert my own.

"You can't even visit your own mother Enzo" I looked up to Enzo with furrowed eye brows.

"I thought you said your mother is sick?" August laughed.

"There's a lot you need to know piccolo, come with me." Enzo kept me behind him.

"Afraid I might tell her about"- in the mist of his words Rebecca Saint came over with her red acrylics.

"Enzo, can we talk?" she his hand on my back and sent me a scowl.

I don't like you either.

"Alone" she crossed her arms.

"I think we all need to have a talk alone" August told my hand leading me away from Enzo and Rebecca. Enzo looked stuck like he couldn't believe that she was right there in front of his eyes, he didn't even stop his father from leading me upstairs.

August brought me to a sealed off room with a chair in side asking me to sit as he sat in front of me.

"Violet Bianchi, let's talk shall we"

□

/□□□□□ □□□ □□ □□□□□□ □□□□□□□□□, □□□□□□ □□□□ □□□□□ □□ □□ □ □□□.

□ □ □ □ □ □ □ □

"□ □ don't think I understand what you're trying tosay" Enzo's father had a menacing laugh, one that would allow your bones to freeze.

"You seem like a smart girl, surely you can comprehend what I'm saying. You end what ever fantasy you and my son have tonight and I'll give you more than he's paying you." he tossed an envelope on the table, it spilled with money inside.

"With all do respect sir, Enzo and I aren't paying for the actual real relationship we have." he snapped his head to me, yanking my hair back in the chair, I winced. His eyes were far different from Enzo, his held nothing but death, everything around him died.

"Do you truly believe, my son would ever love or care for you?" he snickered. "The woman you just saw is his true wife, you are just a whore to him and nothing more." I refused to believe his words.

"You will do nothing but destroy everything he's every worked for." he tugged my arm. "If you believe that I'm going to let you do that you are far from mistaken."

"You are filth in this world Violette." I had never once met someone like his father, everyone seemed to know who I was without me introducing myself. Him knowing my full name wasn't what caught my attention, it was the small note in his hands.

Whoever Rebecca was to Enzo, what ever they had, had to been destroyed in the past. "As long as she's breathing, he will never love you." his grip on my hair became stronger.

"I care for him way more than you believe" I said still wondering what Enzo needed to speak to her about. I stood up fixing my dress.

"You will never be a Romano, you couldn't last a day in his life." I slammed the door not wanting to listen to him anymore. I looked and asked around for Enzo.

No one had seen him, a woman and her husband along with their children greeted me. Their children spitting images of them.

"Mommy she's beautiful" the little girl said.

"I'm Adora, this is my daughter Aria" she waved her small hand at me.

"Violet" Her husband and their son soon joined them. He introduced himself as Reid along with their son Rowan. (□/□ □ □□□□□□ □□ □□□□ □ □□ □□□□ □□□□ □□□□ □□□□ □□□□ □□ □□ □□□□ □□□ □□□□□ □□□□□□□□)

"You must be Enzo's date" she brightly smiled, Reid looked around for him in a questionable manner.

"Are you uncle Enzo's princess?" Aria asked playing with her mother's braid.

"She's too pretty for him Ari" Rowan said with a deep red blush on his face, another little boy by the name of Ace ran over to the young children.

"Ari, will you come play with me? You too Rowan" they all clapped their hands together before running off. Reid still looked in confusion to why Enzo wasn't here next to me but I didn't know either.

They were a very lovely couple, they were so in love. Adora laughed gently at his jokes while laying her head on his chest. I sat next to them smiling when they'd confess their love to one another. I wondered how they met and fell in love gracefully, I wanted a love like theirs, the way the looked into each other's eyes with so much love. Adora's ring was beautiful, Reid adored her and you could see it.

I was starting to anxious, overthinking was something I was good at. When I finally Enzo walk down the white steps with Rebecca she whispered something in his ear before he came over to me.

Jealousy painted on my heart watching her walk off, he sat near me trying to take my hand but I moved it to my lap. He didn't seem fazed by the action, his father soon sat down watching me.

An announcement for Enzo to stand up with me soon came, when everyone joined us at the same time he made sure to keep my hand in his.

When the music started again he led me to the middle of them all, Reid and Adora next to us. Enzo left his hand on my lower hip, my hands on his shoulder I refused to turn my attention to him.

He of course didn't like that, he turned my chin to him. I swept my leg up to his hip as he held it there, he spun me around so my back was against his front.

My hand was on his jaw as he swayed my hips, I was beyond pissed at Enzo. He let her touch him as if he was hers and he hadn't addressed it, then again neither had I.

"Don't think for one second, that I am not mad at you Enzo." he kept his head in my neck. His hand flat on my stomach he kept me flushed on him.

"You're sexy when your mad mi amore" I finally faced him letting him hold my ass in his hands. Keeping up this act would be hard, Enzo was too good with his words.

"I hate you sometimes" in the corner of my eye his father along with Rebecca had pure hate in their eyes for me.

Enzo move my hair to whisper in my ear. "Is that so, do you hate it when I touch you like this?" his hand trailed up the slit of the dress to my inner thigh.

"Enzo..." he hummed against my skin. This point no one could see him from the position we were in, I brushed my knee on his erection making him pause his actions.

My lips grazing his neck. "I do enjoy when you touch me like that, but you love it when I touch you more" the music ended, I walked away moving to the bar with Mariano who seemed extremely happy.

"Gorgeous, you seem angry" he threw his arm around my shoulder.

"It's nothing Mariano."

"How's your lovely mother?" he took a deep gulp of his drink.

"She's awake, I have to visit her tomorrow" he smiled handing me my own drink. Rebecca went to dance with Enzo when he ignored her throwing daggers at Mariano for having his arm around me.

"I have a date.. with Angel tomorrow" he smiled down at the counter. Mariano had freckles that decorated his face wonderfully.

"That's amazing Mariano, I'm so happy for you."

"She's too good for me gorgeous, but her laugh.. you should hear her laugh" Mariano blushed thinking about Angel that made me smile.

"I just want to make her happy." Mariano had a such a good heart, even when he believed that he could never be loved, he didn't see how much she truly cared for him.

"You'll make her the happiest, you're too good for this world Mariano." he hugged my tightly before kissing my forehead.

When he walked away Enzo made his way over to me. Taking my drink he drunk the rest. "My father has been dealt with for what he's said to you." Which must have been true because he was no where to be seen.

I just went into his arms, his arms comforted when I needed them too, the conversation with Rebecca was far from over but I just needed to be with him right now.

"Can we just go home please" The announcer called out for Enzo but he only led us out of the building. The heels were killing my feet, I took them off while Enzo scooped me up holding me until we got inside of the car. Garrett drove us while I laid my head on his chest, he ran invisible shapes on my skin.

Enzo carried me inside of the house removing my makeup along with my clothes. "Enzo.. did you kill Daniel" I knew he did I just had to hear it from him to come to peace with it.

"I did" I nodded closing my eyes. Snuggling into breast he kept me close to him.

"For you mi amore, I'd kill anyone who tries to hurt you" something was still troubling him, I hoped Enzo wasn't thinking of her. If he was I wondered what could have she possibly done to affect him this way.

Enzo let out a long sigh thinking I was asleep but I wasn't. I watched him get up getting dressed once more, kissing my forehead sweetly whispering kind words in my ear.

Then the door shut, I got up running after him but I was too late because he had already left.

"He's not going to her" Damien said standing in the kitchen.

I joined him. "How do you know I was thinking about that?" he shrugged fixing the dishes.

"Because I know my brother, he doesn't care for her Violet. What ever he felt for her died."

"What did she do?" Damien yawned.

"Not my story to tell principessa" He continued up the stairs.

I returned to bed waiting for Enzo, but he hadn't came back all night.

AUGUST stood in his office holding a letter, the letter addressed to Violette Luna Bianchi.

"Who sent this letter" my father grinned taking a seat, spinning in his chair I didn't have time for his games. I wanted no more than to put a bullet through his heart and watch the life drain from his life. The things he said to Violet could have been worst but he was hiding something.

"It was sent to her, but ended on my door step. I wouldn't be worried about who sent it, but who wrote it." he was playing games, just as he always did.

"Sofia would be disappointed in you Enzo, dating a whore." Rage filled my body whenever I spoke to him, nothing ever ended well.

"Don't speak of her" he laughed standing up. Flashes of her eyes filled with crystal lined tears, the blood covering my small hands as I held my hand over her heart. Him standing with the knife in his hands, calling me weak, useless. Her labored breathing finally dying until she closed her eyes.

Why did she close her eyes?

"What, you do remember how she called out for you, what were her last words again Aleksander?"

Forgive me my son.

Purposely shooting the bullet in his left leg, he fell to the ground screaming out in pain. I took the letter placing it in my pocket.

"I will kill her too Enzo, in front of your eyes.. just like Sofia you won't be able to save her."

"Do not mistake me for someone who cares for your life August, I won't hesitate to end your life if you come near her" I slammed the door leaving him to bleed out until someone found him. I didn't need to protect Violet, I wanted too.

The letter fell from my pocket. I reached down for it.

My Sweet Violette.

□

/□ □□□□□□□ □□□□ □□□□□□□ □□ □□□□ □□□□□. □□□□ □□□ □□□□□□□ <3

□ □ □ □ □ □ □

□ □□□□□ last night Enzo had been distant, not even Mariano would tell me who exactly Rebecca was to Enzo. I was sitting in on his bed watching him pace around yelling into his phone.

Enzo stressfully pulled at his hair. I stood up holding my arms around his waist, surprisingly his came around my own, I looked up to him with a small pout. "Do you still care for her?" he looked down at me in irritation.

"I have a right to know Enzo, I need to know so I don't sit here wanting you when you still care for her" his thumb traced my lower hip.

"I do not care for Rebecca, Violet the only woman I do care for.." he laid on his back keeping me on his lap. "She's right in front of me."

"I'm yours Violet, every second of they day. Whenever you want, wherever I'm yours" My hands played with the waist band of his sweats.

"I need you Enzo" I heard his breath hitch, he watched me intently. I dragged my nails down his naked chest over the tattoos.

His lips parted when I leaned over leaving my trail of hickey's on his skin. The image of Rebecca touching Enzo only controlled me more to leave more on his neck, Enzo held my hips as they subconsciously moved down on his. I earned a throaty groan from him when I continued to move them.

"Violet" he removed my shirt palming my breast, his touch alone set my skin to burn. His palm flat on my stomach Enzo's blue eyes ran over my face before he showed his dimpled smile.

Moving between his opened legs Enzo's eyes watched me with hooded lids, removing his neediness from his sweats I used my hand to run up and down his girth. My thumb teased his tip making him lift his hips.

My own hand between my thighs coating my fingers with my wetness I toyed with my clit watching him get off. "Fuck are you playing with yourself." he ran a hand down his face, his cock thrusting into my mouth. "Cazzo.. you're so good."

"That's it tesoro, let me fuck your mouth" he held my head down making me gag around him.

Enzo moved my hair from my face letting me peer up to him through my lashes, Enzo whispered number of curses into the morning air.

When his hot load slid down my throat, I moved into the bathroom to rebrush my teeth before climbing onto his lap.

"Tell me what's wrong."

"We should go visit your mother" he ignored my previous words. His eyes slowly starting to close, the bags underneath them deepening. I smoothed my hand on his cheek too his jaw, Enzo deeply took a breath leaning into my touch.

"You didn't sleep last night did you?" he closed his eyes. I pressed a kiss too his cheek. "I'll go visit her today, you stay and sleep" I went to get up but he held his arms around me.

"I won't take long, sleep for me Enzo okay" he shut his eyes, a few minutes I felt his soft breathing on my neck. I pulled away from him causing him to stir around a bit before holding onto my pillow. I let my lips stay on his forehead, pushing his hair away from his face.

Enzo's long lashes hitting his cheek bones, his pink lips slightly parted. Strong muscles hugging the pillow that lingered with my scent, I didn't know what I did to deserve such a handsome man but I sure was lucky.

I finished getting ready grabbing the beige coat waiting for me on the chair, his house empty not filled with it's usual maids scattered around.

Garrett opened the door the expensive car allowing me inside. The drive to the hospital short, I opened the door seeing my mother sitting up eating what looks like a full breakfast. Her room was new, it was much larger, the television a flat screen, the view from here beautiful. She had clothes hung up on racks too her liking.

Flowers filled the room with different note cards. All of them reading Enzo's name. I smiled too my self before hugging her. "I like him Violet"

"I like him a lot" I pushed a curl behind her ear, she looked healthier, the nurse entered taking her tray filled with food out.

"He came too visit me, Leo" my heart stopped. "He wants too see you." I stood up shaking my head.

"I don't want too see him." I don't like the idea of my father coming to see her after she just started feeling better. Why was he back? Why did he want to see me? "I don't want him coming too see you, not ever again. He's the reason why your condition got worse." I sat on the edge of the bed.

"He's changed Vio" I couldn't believe it, he's already started to manipulate her once again.

"No he hasn't, he's the same man who left you when you got diagnosed" I felt my self starting to get agitated.

"No baby, he said he left because he was getting money for my treatment" She couldn't even see it, the way he's brainwashed her.

I stood up once again running my hands through my hair. "He left, he has a new family he doesn't give two shits about us. Why can't you see he doesn't love you anymore!" I yelled the last part.

"He's never loved us, because if he did he would stay and take care of you at your lowest" the feeling of cold tears slightly pouring down my face. My voice becoming quieter.

"He's back now Vio, he'll make things right" she tried reaching out for me but I backed away.

It was breaking my heart too see her like this, all she ever wanted was his love. My grandma used to tell me that's the reason that's why she gave birth, that their love wasn't there before me.

My mother had me thinking my father would finally love her. "He's not allowed to come see you anymore."

"I'll come back tomorrow" I placed a sad kiss on her cheek before leaving, I made sure too tell the nurses not to let anyone that wasn't me to go into her room.

I stared out into the cloudy grey sky thinking about him, there had to be a reason why he was back, whatever it was, I wasn't ready too see him.

The door shut waking me up, I hadn't even noticed how long I had been asleep. I fell asleep too the scent of her pillow, the coconut, strawberry scent of her filling my senses. I couldn't even sleep last night, I woke up in cold sweats, images of my mother gasping for the air that was non existent in her lungs.

Violet walked in, her hand in her hair while small anxious tears rolled down her cheeks. I rushed over to her feeling the water pain my heart seeing her like this.

"Who did this to you? I'll kill them" she didn't say anything, she only cried more into my palms, there was no sign of bruises on her skin, her clothes still neat.

"My f-father Enzo.. he went to visit her" her voice became quieter.

"What's his name?" I wiped the tear off of her soft cheeks. God I didn't like seeing her like this,

"L-Leonardo Bianchi why?" she sniffled out the last part but my blood ran cold.

"Enzo what's wrong?" I sent a quick text too Damien too move her mother too our private hospital now. Violet's small footsteps followed me as I opened the closet grabbing my jacket.

"Violet stay here and don't leave this room" just like the stubborn little brat she was she put on her shoes.

Mariano rushed through the door along with Alejandro, Violet jumped seeing the angry looks on their faces.

Snapping my fingers at the six other men that walked in with them too stay here with her.

"Can you please tell me what's going on?" I kept speaking too Alejandro before she grabbed my arm turning me too her. "Why are you guys acting as if I don't exist?" There was a lot Violet didn't know about her father, she didn't like being in the dark but for her safety she had too be.

"Call Valerie and stay here." she rolled her eyes, I left one last kiss on her sweet lips, the lips I wanted too taste forever.

"Enzo, stop doing this. Stop acting like this is the last time we'll see each other" she shoved my chest.

I can't put her through this, not after tonight.

Her sad eyes returned when I didn't say anything. "Enzo" I cut her off.

"Call Valerie and stay inside Violet" was the last thing I said before walking out the doors.

/ I've been working on a new book series. The first book will be called "Playing With Hearts" it won't be out for awhile until this is complete then probably a month after.

□ □ □ □ □ □ □

VALERIE and I currently crying on the couch watching a sad romantic movie, she wanted to get my mind off of Enzo's and hers off of Damien. I didn't know what made Enzo panic after I said my father's name but I was stuck with no answers yet millions of questions.

I looked at the time it was almost midnight and no word from anyone, the guards just standing by the doors with heavy guns in their hands and on their sides

"Men can kiss my ass" Did I mention we got extremely drunk? Valerie's mascara was running down her cheek, she stood on the chair yelling at the screen making me laugh.

I stumbled up to the kitchen getting the ice cream carton when Enzo, Damien, Mariano and Alejandro strummed inside with pissed expressions. Valerie tripped on her feet falling into Damien's arms.

"Cazzo, are you drunk Val?" she shook her head.

"Drunk?.. me I would never do such thing" she stuck her finger in his face. Enzo came over to me holding my jaw.

"I can't deal with this right now" he said moving away from me going upstairs. I followed after him, before he could close the door I slipped inside of the door.

Enzo was removing his shirt, his back muscles contracting with each movement. "Enzo, can you please say something" he removed his watch.

"You're drunk Violet." I cursed myself for feeling horny when he turned around only in his pants low on his waist. I was sober enough to want to speak to him.

"Can you just tell me what happened?"I wasn't even allowed to leave to visit my mother to ask her either.

Enzo's eyes only burned with anger, he looked at me like my father was standing in front of him and not me. "Violet, go to sleep" I took a step closer to him.

"I'm getting sick of you acting as if we aren't in this together, you kiss me like you were going to leave me, you come back and give me no answers. Stop pushing me away Enzo" I hugged my arms around his torso, placing a gentle kiss to his back meeting the tattoo there.

Enzo's body stilled for a second before moving away from me. The smallest action making my heart dropped. "You're drunk Violet" he entered the bathroom.

"Stop using that stupid fucking excuse and talk to me" He ignored me further, my attention fell upon a small note that fell from his pocket earlier, I picked up going to return it to him when the letter stated my name at the top.

I sat back on the bed as Enzo stood by the bathroom sink running a hand down his face.

My Sweet VioletteYou've grown more than I remember, I've been watching you more than you know. Both of you in fact, your mother seems to be doing so well. She tells me that you don't believe that I love you, that is where you're wrong Violette. I never left because I didn't love you, I left because I simply didn't love her. You on the other hand are my daughter, who I will love dearly.

Forever will I love you Violette, but tell me. I know you aren't the one paying for all those expenses cost of your mother's tragic illness, I know this because I left you with absolutely nothing, nothing without me, you will always be nothing. I'm going to find you, and remind you again, you do remember those nights don't you?

When I find out who is letting you believe that peace is finally at your hands. I'm going to kill them, I'm going to kill every one who's ever made you smile that wasn't me.

I mentally cursed myself for taking everything out of Violet. The bathroom door was now closed, behind it was mixed in silence, I finally got out the shower dreading having to open this door. Scared of what I'll say next to upset her.

The whole thing was a set up, just like Leonardo wanted was to play games, using Violet as a pawn. Damien was able to do more research about Leonardo and their names background. She's of the Italian descendant, that would make her as important as I was to my mafia, downside was Leo didn't have one. Not with his child. He was on the search for her, only to get what he wanted and that was power, but I wouldn't let him take the only person who mattered to me.

I opened the door expecting her to be asleep, Violet held the note in her hands, a single tear dropped her her brown eyes down to the white paper. Her hands shaking at the note until she looked up at me. Crumbling it up, she wiped the tear.

"He's coming for me" she stood up, the long grey t shirt hitting her thighs.

"He's coming for me" she repeated lowly to herself. Violet clutched her curls in her hand pacing back and forth. Closing her eyes tightly she fell to the floor, whispering words in the letter. Her breathing picked up in the worse ways, she held a hand to her heart.

I fell to the floor next to her pulling her onto my lap, lifting her head to me. Swirling in the depths of her brown eyes laid fear, tears and pain. "E-Enzo he's going to kill me."

"Look at me Violet" she shook her head no as her breathing became unstable. "Tesoro, I need you to breathe." I wasn't good with this stuff, but I would try for her.

I wiped the fallen tears off her beautiful skin, she held her head in my neck trying to call herself down, I ran my hand down her back comforting, my other hand running circles around her hip. Something I learned she likes to help her sleep.

I held her face in the palms of my hands, I couldn't bare seeing her this way, afraid. "I would never let him get to you." her hand held my own.

"You don't get it Enzo, he won't just kill me, he'll kill my mother... he'll kill you." her eyes widened at her words, she wrapped her arms around me tightly. "I won't lose you Enzo, I can't lose her"

"He doesn't want me to be happy, he feels the need to destroy everything, and every one I love" I don't think Violet realized what she said, neither did my brain process her words. I was too focused on reassuring her.

"Look at me tesoro" I soothed my thumb on her cheeks. I placed a kiss to her forehead.

"The last thing I would do, is let anyone hurt you. I promise you, I'm going to protect you, no matter the cost" she kept quiet, her tears now dried on her soft skin, her breathing finally coming back to it's normal state.

Violet kept her hand on my heart the whole night, her leg on top of my own. Arm draped over my waist like she was scared I would disappear at a snap of a finger. Her perfect lips parted, her small breaths hitting my neck, eyebrows furrowed at a bad dream.

When I went to move she clung to me more, I hated how bad he affected her even when I didn't know the story, there was more too it than him just leaving her.

It almost tore me apart when I told Violet that I had something to do, she almost had a panic attack but Mariano promised not to leave her side.

I didn't bother knocking on the door, Violet's mother stood at the window with the tube connecting to her arm.

"You knew didn't you." she turned to face me with an identical note in her hand.

"I'm going to ask you one last time and if you know what's good for you, you'll tell me the truth."

"When did he actually come visit you?" She went to open her mouth but replaced it with a smile.

"Leo has always been around, watching her that is. Do you remember Daniel? The poor man you killed. Why do you think he was always so persistent to Violette?"

"Your daughter was working in a shit hole trying to save your fucking life."

"My daughter is the reason my husband doesn't love me." I laughed, searching the room for any signs of anyone else being in here before me. There was none.

Was it wrong that I wanted to pull the chord that was keeping her from standing right now?

"You've read the note, the only reason Leo is back is because of her. Tell me then" I sat down on the chair.

"You're a smart women aren't you? You can see it clear as day he only truly loves her, he never has and never will love you, face it" I could see her anger building up.

"T-that's is not true, Leo despises her." I removed the folder from the back of my suit.

Her eyes widened with panic. "You're a conniving bitch you know that."

"All these years you let her believe that you were sick, and in need of money. Allowing her to take nothing but shit from assholes, when in reality you aren't even her fucking mother" she snapped her head to the window. I took my stand grabbing her by the neck.

"I'm going to have a fun time watching your blood spill all over this floor."

"Do you honestly believe that she'll forgive you, for killing the only person she's ever had. She's going to hate you Enzo, despise you for the scum that you truly are. She will never forgive you" she smiled in triumph.

It fell when I placed my gun tapping it on her temple. Killing her would break Violet, she didn't know the truth behind her fucked up family it would only break her further. I couldn't stand by letting every thing around her fall, I wouldn't let it happen.

Her hands clung to the window curtains. "That's where you're wrong." I let the gun press deeper in her neck.

"She has me now, she has me forever."

Mariano invited Angel over and my heart warmed for him. The pink tint on his cheeks never faltered, she could simply take a long breath in and he'd blush at her simplest acts.

She was the sweetest person ever, even with her own deep colored skin you could see her blushing at his teasing acts. I got up to leave them alone, I waited for Enzo to come back after he left. He told me there was nothing to be worried about, that he wouldn't let anything happen to me. I wanted him to be safe too. Loud banging came from downstairs, I went to open the door when it was already done for me.

One of the guard barged through the doors trying to call me to follow him but he was too late. I screamed from the top of my voice box when his body fell limply to the ground, blood pouring from the back of his head.

Someone slowly dragging the gun on the wall entered. Stepping over the lifeless body, he turned his head to me.

Please no.

There he was with the same scar over his face, the black eyes that never once saw light. The low cut black hair with minimal curls. Another loud crash came from downstairs.

I heard Angel's crying from downstairs, Mariano groaning loudly before it stopped.

"Get away f-from me" I tried to run to do something but my legs were glued to the floor.

"That's a shitty way to welcome back your own father don't you think."

<3/ I've been so busy this week excuse my messy update times. I seriously don't know how to feel about this book anymore..

□ □ □ □ □ □ □ □ □

All that was heard throughout my ears was the loud ringing of my the bullet piercing through the man's neck, stopping his veins from letting any blood flow to his heart, the same sound that made me smile when the woman pretending to be Violet's mother fell to the floor, I tore the whole house trying to find her until Damien told me about Leonardo.

Mariano being shot close to his heart was hanging on for dear life in the hospital. Angel hadn't left his side since then.

Alejandro telling me to stop wasn't helping. All I saw was Leonardo's face, my Violet's eyes laced in fear at his hands.

When I said there was more to the story I wasn't lying. Violet's mother was still alive, she left her with Leonardo because she herself was scared of what the man could do to her, all her life he blamed her for the disappearance of his wife. Days and nights he'd torment her with his words, Violet suffered far worse then I could imagine.

Violet's records showed her being sent to emergency care due to blood force trauma.Body covered in now healed bruises, scars along her back to her thighs. Violet suffered severe amnesia at the age of seven causing her to forget the traumatic events.

When in search of Leonardo, they came up dry. Only left with the woman who claimed to be her mother they let her case go incomplete.

"You need to calm down, We'll find her" Reid said to the side of me.

"Calm down? You think I can be calm when she's out there scared out of her fucking mind!"

"What I've learned is that she's strong Enzo" Ryan said to the other side. I know my Violet is strong but she's been broken before, how long would it last until she was completely destroyed?

"I didn't think I would have to ever coming back to using one of these" he emptied the clip.

"Alright fuckers, listen here. Reid I don't want you hurting yourself with one of those, I'm not trying to get cussed out by a pregnant Adora" Jax patted Reid's back.

"Adora's scary even when she's not pregnant" Jax grabbed the gun from Reid.

"Hey asshole, that's my sister in law your talking about" Ryan pointed the gun to Jax.

"Do us all a favor Ryan, stop eating all the fucking ice cream." I groaned at the constant bickering.

"I'm going to kill every single one of you if you don't help me find her."

"And I'm going to kill you if you keep talking about my wife like that" Reid said to Jax.

"Calm down old man, I wouldn't want you to throw your back out" I threw Violet's phone on the table. I couldn't be here with them, I got into the car driving the club I hadn't been in over a month.

Helena ran to me throwing her arms over me, I shoved her off making her fall onto the floor. "Enzo.. I've missed you" her black hair now with brown streaks.

The only thing on my mind was seeing that beautiful smile Violet wore proudly when she was around me. I slammed the door shut before Helena could enter, my office being kept fresh laid a small note on the table.

Times ticking Romano. Seems like I've triggered an old memory of hers.

A small disc was playing on the laptop, when I pressed play, Violet was tied strictly to a chair, her legs filled with scars, crimson blood falling slowly down her cheek, her eyes shut tightly until Leo pulled her hair back. He stabbed her left thigh with a knife she screamed out in pain.

"She's been saying your name since she's got her. To be quite honest I can't stand it."

Her eyes swollen with tears constant streaming from her eye. "P-Please stop"

Leonardo yanked at her hair harder making her look into the camera, her body only covered in my grey shirt.

"Tell him what you said." she refused.

"Fine then I will" he walked in front of the camera. "My sweet daughter here chose your life over her own, she'd rather you live then her."

"Enzo"- he cut off the video before she could say what she needed to. I threw the laptop at the wall allowing it to crash. I heard the sound of Damien yelling at everyone to get out.

"Even if it kills me we will find her" he said as they all loaded the black cars with different varieties of guns.

That goes for me to. Damien was able to track the location but we were taking every precaution, there was no way Leonardo would allow us to find him just like that.

We got constant updates about Mariano, they were still trying to get him stable.

"This doesn't feel right" Ryan said as he opened the doors. This was the place, the single chair was sitting in the middle of it all, the constant sound of Violet crying rung around the room.

"Enzo" her weak voice called out before it finally stopped, there was nothing but pure red in my eyes, I wanted to kill him, directly in his heart and watch him die in front of me.

He wasn't stupid enough to kill her, I discarded those thoughts from my head. I promised Violet that I wouldn't let anything happen to her, I promised I would kill anyone who hurt her even if it killed me. Damien came out telling us that there wasn't anyone here. August walked down from the steps grinning.

"Beautiful girl by the way, Sophia would have loved her" he twirled his finger around in the air.

I wasted no time pulling him by his neck, he laughed then those laughs turned into unbearable coughs. "She doesn't seem to like broken glass through"

"Where the fuck is she?" he looked around before my phone rung in my pocket. My fist were tightening around his throat, the beating in my heart continued to pump blood in ever vein in my body.

"Maybe you should pick that up" I dropped him to the floor, he coughed up blood onto the floor, I kneeled down next to him holding his hair back, shoving the gun into his mouth I leaned into his ear.

"You talk about slow and painful deaths, how they help you sleep at night. Nothing would be better than to see you lying here as your heart" I pushed my gun further into his chest. "Stops, your blood, spilling from your worthless body."

"S-She will never love you" he choked on his words, the loud bullet flew directly in his chest, stopping his heart all at once. August's lifeless body fell from my grasp, his blood was the scent around the room. The phone in my pocket rang constantly.

"What" I shouted, the voice behind the phone squeaked.

"E-Enzo" her voice, her voice was quiet, and strained from the all the yelling. "P-Please"

"Tell me where you are Violet" I hurried to the car, I could hear the unsteady breathing coming from the end of the line. "Tesoro talk to me."

"I-I'm at my place" her sniffles and short cries only tore at my heart more, I told Reid to hurry up and drive, I kept her own the phone.

"It hurts E-Enzo" when he parked I left them in car running into the opened building, the beating in my heart grew when her door was broken down. I tossed the phone into the room ready to run to her but stopped in my tracks.

Shattered glass surrounded Violet as she sat in the middle, her knees hugged tightly too her chest, her black curls sprawled over her shoulders. Her soft skin now cut up on her legs, she lifted her head to me, the once bright glint in her eyes now replaced with pain. I pushed the glass away from her, holding her into my arms, her cheeks in my palms. The cold tears fell from her eyes to my hands.

"It hurts so much" she motioned towards her body, her tears spilling more. Fuck I couldn't see her like this, her beautiful face now being accompanied by a scar on her cheek.

She closed her arms tightly around my neck, her head resting in the crook. "Please don't let go" her sobbing continued. I picked her up, her legs closing around me tightly. "Please" her voice cracked.

"Find him" I told Damien who nodded, they didn't say anything seeing her state. I held her in my lap the whole time in the car, when we made it home I called the nurse to clean up her bruises. Violet refused to let go of my body as I sat her in the bathroom counter.

Her body shaking in trauma, eyes closed tightly. I was going to do more than kill Leonardo for what he did, more than torture.

The nurse came in asking Violet to show her, her arm but she refused to speak to her. "I want to sleep" she said in my neck in a whisper.

"I know tesoro, let me do then hm?" she nodded, I used the burning liquid to lightly clean her new profound scars, she kept her head down not looking at me. I dismissed the nurse.

She winced when I finished the last one that seemed deeper than the others. The warm water welcomed her as she closed her eyes, she held on my hand when I went to get her a towel.

"I'm going to kill him Violet" she didn't say anything, anxiously biting her lip she rose her gaze to me.

"He told me you killed her" I let her continue. "Thank you" The guilt that was eating at my heart faded, I don't know what I would have done if she was truly mad at me.

She got up wrapping the grey towel around her frame, resting her forehead on my own she placed a loving kiss on my lips. Dammit I missed these lips, I missed her.

"Are you okay?" she asked weakly as I laid her sore body in the bed, I removed the towel pressing my lips to her neck, dressing her into my white shirt.

"I was thinking"- she cut me off holding my face, bringing our lips together, the sweet taste returned to my mouth.

"Don't think about him, or anyone. Just be here with me" She wanted to say something but just continued to bite her lip.

She soon she fell asleep, her legs tangled in with mine. Her heartbeat slowing down as I stroked the side of her arm with the pads of her fingers.

Enzo was speaking to Damien upstairs, I was in the kitchen cooking with Adora, her children sat in the chairs playing with their toys.

"Ace can you be my boyfriend?" Aria asked the small blushing boy.

"Fu"- Adora shot Reid a glare.

"Absolutely not" he picked his daughter up as she frowned in his arms being taken away from her friend. "You are not allowed to have a boyfriend."

"But mommy said I could" Adora whistled in the air avoiding the eyebrow Reid just rose at her.

"Everyone has a boyfriend but me" she huffed, her eyebrows deepening her pout.

"Mommy, how did papa become your boyfriend?" Adora choked on the water in her hand before clearing her throat.

She picked up Aria spinning her in the air making her laugh. "Remember when I told you, the story about the princess who was saved from the ugly creature who loved his mother more" she nodded excitedly.

"And papa saved you from him!"she clapped her small hands together. Aria was definitely Adora's twin, from their deep skin, the curls that framed their faces, to the sun colored brown eyes.

"Did uncle Enzo save you from an ugly man?" Rowan said next to me playing with the toy car.

"He did in fact."

"Do you love him like my mommy loves my papa?" Aria sat on the counter at the same time Enzo came from the steps, in an all black suit, his hair styled as it always was, the tattoos on his hand being showcased along with his biceps that flexed with the smallest movements.

"I do love him" I admitted to her, as he came over lifting her up.

"Little flower" he tickled her stomach.

I love Enzo.

/ small update before I go to bed!

□ □ □ □ □ □ □

A week since everything happened. Leonardo had been silent since then but Enzo knew it was too good to be true and he was planning something.

I watched Enzo empty the clip of the gun before tucking it in the waist band of his pants. Enzo told me my real mother was still alive and I didn't want to speak about it so he left it alone.

If she cared about me she would have made an effort too see me.

Enzo was practicing shooting at a target, his white shirt fully unbuttoned, the tie around his neck laying on his chest showing off his beautiful body. Enzo directly shot the target between its eyes before turning his attention too me.

I would be lying if I said it wasn't hot to watch him do this. "Come here" I hurried over to him.

He stood me in front of him, his kept his hands on my waist making sure I was looking forward. "Can you teach me?" he held my arm out.

The gun felt heavy in my palms, he held my waist with one hand and the other pointed the gun towards the forehead of the dummy. "Relax for me tesoro" I let out a deep breath.

My finger pulled the trigger, the impact of the gun making me fall back into Enzo's chest. The bullet hole went straight into the eyes.

I turned around with a smile on my face only too be met with the hooded eyes of blue.

"I want to do it again" I excitedly said but he removed the weapon from my grasp.

"We have more important things too take care of" he took my hand leading me away from the dark warehouse.

Another room with hangers filled of short dresses hung along them. "Enzo, what's this" he held my chin close to him.

"You know I would never put you in danger correct?" I nodded. "Use your words Violet" he said in a serious tone.

"I know you wouldn't" he layered a kiss to my lips.

"Helena's father owns his own mafia, it's weak which leads us to believe he's part of the reason why Leonardo found you, he's been hiding from me. But if he hears that Leonardo let you go, he'll come out and take you for himself."

"You don't have to do this Violet, we can find someone else" he sensed my unsure ness. He cupped my cheek with his right hand. "But if you agree too do this, I'm going to need you too listen too me the whole time" I thought about it, but if I was going to be apart of Enzo's life, I would have to get used to the jobs that came along with it.

I loved him, the love for him answered for me. "I'll do it'" he searched for any signs of hesitation but nodded when he sat me down on the chair.

Snapping his fingers one of the maids came running in. "Get her ready, and go with the black dress" she addressed him as boss as he walked out of the door.

After she finished doing my makeup, I ran my hands down the side of the tight body cotton black dress, the v line of the neck exposed more of my chest, the dress was short also showing off my mid thighs.

She informed me Enzo was waiting for me downstairs, Mariano was first to see me. His arm in cast as he welcomed me into his arms.

"Mariano! I missed you so much" then I pushed his chest. "That's for scaring me half to death" Mariano was finally out of the hospital, I wasn't able to visit him because he had been in surgery since he got there.

"I missed you too gorgeous, you didn't think I would leave you without saying goodbye did you?" I missed his playful demeanor.

"Enzo's waiting for you in the car" I thanked Garrett as he opened the door for me.

I sat next to Enzo as the window closed di ding the driver from hearing or seeing us.

Enzo trailed his eyes from my perfectly shaven legs up to my exposed chest. "Fuck" he said scooting me closer to him, Enzo looked good himself. His black suit buttoned up all the way, the gold watch on his tattooed wrist.

"You don't look half bad yourself Mr. Romano." he turned my chin to him.

"You, Mrs. Romano. Look beautiful as always" My heart fluttered at his words, he placed a sweet kiss to the back of my hand before he became serious.

He placed a ring on my finger. "It's a mic, with this I'll be able to hear your whole conversation."

"With the father right?"

"No, with his son. Estefano is his involvement is useless but he's young so it'll be easier to get information out about him" I admired the shiny diamond, though it was fake I couldn't help about think about the day it would be replaced with a real one.

"He's never seen your face before, you'll seduce him until he ask to take you upstairs. Don't worry we'll be there before he can try anything. But I need you to be careful, the men at the casino are dangerous, do not take any drinks unless they come from the Alejandro who will act like the bartender" I nodded as the car stopped.

Enzo lifted up my dress attaching a black band with a knife on its side to my thigh. The knife read my name. My full name in a cursive font.

I kissed his lips deeply before we stepped out. "Ready?" No.

"Yes" How hard could it be to seduce a man that was barely twenty one.

Enzo and I entered making all the heads whip too us, they all greeted him with respect and bowing their heads. He led us to the bar where we met Alejandro who sent me a wink.

"I always knew you were bad ass, peaches" he said pouring me a fruit drink.

"They all believe we're married so make sure too show off your ring" I lightly sipped on the drink watching all the men's and women's eyes watching me darkly.

Maybe the slit in on this dress was too high, but judging the way Enzo couldn't remove his hand from my thigh I guess it was perfect.

"Then if you marry me, you can take me on a honey moon can't you" I said in his ear looking direct eye contact with the man that resembled Helena.

"When Violet" I furrowed my eyebrows at him.

"When I marry you" he acknowledged my hint that Estefano was here and already watching me.

My heart beat picked up, at the thought of Enzo and I being married. Me becoming his wife, I hadn't even built up the courage too tell him that I love him.

"Remember" he kissed my cheek. "Don't let him touch what's mine" I rolled my eyes as he walked off.

I finished my drink when a hand placed on my lower back. "I've never seen you around here before" Estefano said with his thumb caressing my hip.

"Shame isn't it" he saw my empty glass.

"Give her another" he pushed the glass towards Alejandro before looking at me. "And make it.. special" Alejandro turned his back whispering something in his mic before he transferred into my own mic in my ear.

"You're going to have to pretend as if the drink is drugged" How bad I wanted to punch the man next to me for thinking he could drug me so easily.

I took a large gulp of the drink as Estefano watched the last drop hit my lips. "I don't believe I've gotten your name"

I stood up on my feet meeting the green in his eyes. "You can call me.. Violette" I said with a thick accent that was inherited from my father.

"Estefano, but you may call me Stefan" be shortened his name. Then I acted as if my eyes were slowly dropping close.

"Are you okay?" he said with a smirk.

"M-My head hurts that's all."

"Let me help you" he held my waist harshly, moving us past the crowd, too a dark way up the stairs.

"Atta girl peaches, sucker doesn't know what's coming to him" Alejandro said in my ear.

Stefano's fingers dug into my side making me wince as he cooed me to shut up. "We're going to have so much fun tonight" he brought us into a room locking the door.

I pretended not to hear his voice, acting as if my body was limp. He pushed me onto the bed, as he poured himself a glass of water.

"I've never had anyone so willing to take a drink, I guess all whores are dumb aren't they" he said in a victory voice while his back was facing me.

He took off his suit jacket coming over too me, he yanked my hair making me let out an inaudible cry. "If you were with Enzo Romano, you must be worth a lot of money" he ripped the front of my dress, I whispered into the mic for Enzo but nothing came out the other end.

"Enzo" I said faintly.

"He can't save you" I felt disgusted as he kissed on my neck, I couldn't sit around and wait for Enzo even as his hand went up my thigh.

I removed the blade from underneath my dress, I flipped him so I was on top of him. He seemed taken back trying to figure out why I wasn't passed out.

He reached up to choke me which he succeeded. Then he turned us over stopping the air from flowing from my lungs, I lodged the knife into his side of his ribs making him stagger back.

"You bitch" he fell onto the floor. I roughly pulled the knife his body, sticking it into his hand. He cried out in pain like a little bitch when I repeated the action into his left hand.

I tugged his head up by his hair so he could look at me. "I'd rather be a dumb whore, then a dead one" I said before my heels connected with his nose knocking him unconscious.

Then the door flew open. "Took you long enough" I said too Alejandro who looked at the scene in front of him. I cleaned off the knife on Stefano's jacket.

"I didn't want to get this dirty, it's just too pretty" Then Enzo walked in ready to kill him but froze when he saw his body.

Enzo them looked up to me, there wasn't shock in his eyes they only darkened in lust.

"Wait for me in the car" he said snapping his fingers as six other guys walked in to help Estefano up into the chair.

I pressed a kiss to his cheek. "When I call your name Enzo, I expect you to be here at the exact second. I almost broke a nail" then I walked off.

I'm not sure what the hell came over me, but I liked it. The odd smile raised on my lips as I looked at the blade in my hand, I stuck it back in its place on the hand on my thigh. I asked Garrett too take me home not bothering to wait for Enzo.

...

I was sitting on the bed with the black silk robe on my body when Enzo opened the door.

His white shirt drenched in blood that wasn't his. I removed it giving me the view of his beautiful body. He ran a hand down his face before sighing, I got up wanting to hug him but he seemed so tense.

Instead he turned to me, the evil glint in his eyes returned. "I didn't think you had it in you tesoro, to be quite frank I was turned on."

"So you're saying you saw"-

"There was a camera in the room" I shoved him in his chest making him laugh.

"It's not funny Enzo, what if I was a helpless person and couldn't fight for myself!" I exclaimed pushing him into the door.

He grabbed my wrist pulling me flushed against him, he held my cheek with his right hand. "But you aren't a helpless person Violet, no helpless person knows how to round house kick someone in the jaw. No helpless person knows how to shoot a gun on their first try."

"I want you to train me then, you aren't always going to be around to save me. I want to learn to fend for myself" he agreed with the nodding of his head.

"That's where you're wrong, I'm always going to be around." the room fell silent.

"Enzo I"- Loud yelling came from downstairs cutting me off.

We went to go see what was happening.

"You killed my brother" Helena dropped to the floor crying. Enzo rolled his eyes asking his guards to carry her out.

I didn't know whether to feel bad or not, I did stab her brother. Enzo held my chin. "Don't feel bad for him tesoro, he deserved more than what I gave him" he said when she saw us.

"You, you fucking bitch" she tried running at me until Mariano caught her with his not injured arm.

"I'm going to kill you, you dirty slut!" she spat at me making Mariano drop her to her knees.

"Use her until she gives us information on her father" Alejandro pointed out. Helena's face dropped into fear.

"N-no please, I don't know where he is" she pleaded with Enzo but he was too busy kissing my shoulder.

"How about we have some fun?" he said in my ear. I held his hand as the dragged her to the back of the house where Enzo did all his torturing.

"If you want me to teach you, this will be your first lesson."

"Which is not to feel any remorse."

...

/ sorry for late updates & the constant cliff hangers, actually I'm not sorry for the cliff hangers but I still love you all. If there are errors it's because I'm half asleep and will edit them later.

□ □ □ □ □ □ □ □

"Do you see him?" Alejandro said as I sat on the side of him. My vision was turned to the man on the couch, dark tanned skin, brown eyes and muscles ready to be set free from his shirt. "Do your thing peaches."

The sound of the music seemed to subside as I entered his private booth. He kept his arms on either side of the couch, I took my seat on his lap letting both my legs sit on either side of him.

"Ivano Ramirez" He seemed taken back that I knew his name, but Ivano was a type of man who liked when woman spoke highly of him. To feed his fat ego.

The black curtains closed around us, he moved his hands down to my waist. "I must know your name if you know mine."

I leaned in his ear, leaving a trail of my lips down his jaw. "Violette" Enzo warned through the mic in my ear.

"Just doing my job." I responded but Ivano was too lost in the kiss that I placed on his neck.

"You are not going to be good for me" he said rubbing all over my ass.

I made my lower half brush Ivano's, he let out a throaty curse in my ear. I tugged on his hair to lean his head to the side, the red of my lipstick sticking to his dark skin.

I closed my legs tighter around his sides to feel if he had a gun, when I felt it on the waist band of his pants, I kept letting him play with my breast through the flimsy outfit.

"Violette hurry up" Enzo said getting irritated. I looked up to the camera knowing he was watching up and blew him a kiss.

Easily removing the gun from his pocket, I kicked it underneath the curtains. I grabbed his jaw seeing him flutter his brown eyes open, to far gone in my ecstasy.

The sparkling dust on my lips transferred to his when I placed the final kiss on his own. Ivano seemed to want more until his arms fell off my body and his eyes shut. I checked his pulse to feel him passed out.

"Good job gorgeous!" Mariano shouted through the mic.

I went up the steps the door where Enzo was watching everything, when I opened the door he lifted his gaze towards me. "You didn't have to kiss him that much" I rolled my eyes sitting on his desk.

He placed his hands on my bare thighs. I wiped the remaining of the fairy like dust on my lips off along with my makeup. I pulled my hair into a tight bun getting off the desk. I undressed my self changing into the tight burgundy cocktail dress, the neck line deeper than I would like, it barely hid any of my breast.

"He doesn't get to touch you" Enzo said coming up behind me, he turned me around backing me into the wall.

"Jealous are we Enzo?" Enzo went to try and leave a mark on my neck but I stopped him. "Can't have them thinking I'm not available" his jaw clenched.

"That's because you aren't." then his teasing smirk appeared. He pulled me towards him, taking the hold on my neck. His lips were close to mine making me bit my own.

"No matter how many people look at you tonight tesoro, you are mine" then he took a handful of my ass. "Now go out there and behave" the deepness in his voice only turned me on further.

I walked to the door turning swiftly on my heels. "No promises" then I closed it.

A couple weeks since Estefano died along with Helena. Since then Enzo wouldn't stop showing me how to defend myself in situations, Mariano's lessons and Alejandro's, it felt like they were trying to make me into a torture slut.

The images of Helena calling out for me to bring mercy on her brought a smile to my face.

"Please! I don't know where he is" she cried trying to fight against the ropes.

Enzo's sinister smirk made her avert her eyes over to me. "Y-You have to believe me"

Enzo came up behind me lifting the knife to her cheek that was still in her hand. When he moved it by her neck he placed it directly on her vein.

"Isn't it funny, one single poke and she's dead" He said more to me than Helena, her eyes was shut tightly.

My chest was rising and falling but it wasn't because I was scared, Enzo was whispering in my ear, his fingers lightly ran down my arm.

"She's lying" he gestured for me to continue. "She knows where he is.. where they both are."

"Her heart beat skips every time and it's not because of the blade." That seemed to angrier Enzo as he pressed it deeper in her vein then taking out his gun in his other hand.

"I don't like liars Helena" I lifted the knife to her cheek. "Lets not make this harder than it has to be" I started to sound like Enzo.

"He's been watching you for a while and you haven't even noticed" Then she looked to Mariano in the back who creased his eyebrows together.

"Angel is such a nice girl, what a shame she works for my father" Mariano walked over to her gripping her hair in her hands.

"What the fuck are you talking about" Helena laughed.

"You didn't believe she would actually like you did you Mariano? Angel was sent to get close to Violet and what better way than to get close to the person she trust. How do you think Leonardo got into the house they day you got shot" I could see Mariano's anger coming from his eyes, he cursed loudly letting the echo bounce off the walls.

I didn't let her mess with his head anymore before I stabbed the knife into her thigh making her cry out in pain. I ripped it out wiping her blood onto her cheek before Enzo pulled the trigger.

Mariano hadn't heard from Angel since, it's like she disappeared from the world. He apologized to me every chance he got because he believed it was his fault but I assured him it wasn't.

Her real name wasn't even Angel, if it was she didn't exist.

"Give the lady another drink" Valentino said coming over to me.

"My husband won't like this" That intrigued him as he lit the cigarette in his mouth.

"What he doesn't know won't hurt him" he winked lifting he glass to my lips.

"I hope he doesn't mind sharing" his hand ran over my ass. I could practically see Enzo clenching his jaw right now.

"Not one bit" Valentino raised an eyebrow as I took his hand leading him up the stairs. In the dark hall way, I began to kiss his dry lips. He pushed me against the wall as his tongue entered my mouth, I slipped the pill into his.

"Let's go in here it's more.. private" He nodded following me into the room. The pill seemed to be working because his eyes started to flutter close.

I pushed him onto the bed as Enzo opened the door. "I'll be sure to cut his hands off for touching what's mine."

Valentino was out cold as I tied his wrist up, I grabbed the ice bucket filled with cold water pouring it on top of his head as he woke up in an instant.

"Nice to see you again Romano." Enzo smirked rolling up his sleeves.

"You must really care for the whore don't you?" He laughed looking at me. "All this trouble for his daughter, you're really something special."

"Your wife.. Isadora I think it was. Lovely woman, speak so highly about the father of her children" he took out a photo card of his children.

Enzo forced Valentino took look at the photo. "It's his birthday soon isnt it? What better gift than his father's head personally delivered to him.. what was his name, Dylan? it was it Vincent. I can't ever keep up with how many times your remarried."

"You leave my family out of this" That's when Enzo chuckled darkly.

He took out his gun patting his cheek with it. "I don't usually like threatening loved ones" he gripped his chin turning it towards me. "But for her, I would kill every soul that tries to take her from me" I was fucking blushing right now as he winked at me.

Damn you Enzo Romano.

"Now be good for her and tell me where he is" Valentino sighed before giving in.

"Spain, they went to Spain" Enzo creased his eyebrows together.

"What's in Spain?" I found myself asking.

"Not what princess, who."

from days of writers block, I was able to write a prologue for my new book.

next chapter is in progress. chapter thoughts?

▯ ▯ ▯ ▯ ▯ ▯

Enzo was in a white shirt that was loosely unbuttoned at the top, we had been on the plane for a while now and not once have my legs stop pressing themselves together.

His blue eyes looked at me as they pulled their attention away from laptop on his lap.

"Is there something wrong tesoro?" It's been weeks since we last had sex and I was growing impatient, Enzo has been extremely busy.

I got out of my seat closing the door and locking it from any of the employees from getting in.

"Violette" he warned as I unbuttoned his shirt. I put my finger to his lips to shut him up.

"No, no more I'm busy. You're going to shut up and let me ride you on this plane" he rose his eyebrow at me before compiling.

Unbuckling his pants, Enzo was already incredibly hard for me. He removed my shirt throwing it on the seat behind me as I sunk down onto him. He cursed in Italian in my ear before telling me to move my hips or he was going to go mad.

Enzo held my head to the side as he hungrily pressed heated to my neck, his warm tongue laid flat on my skin as he continued to mark the spot.

My nails clawing at his shoulders he threw his head back before moaning my name. I pulled his hair for him to look into my eyes. "First time having sex on a plane?" I shook my head which made him pinch my hip.

I leaned into his ear before biting down on it. "First time I've had sex on your plane, now try and be quiet when you come for me" he bounced down onto him faster as his hand found it's spot onto my neck bringing our lips together.

He landed a smack onto my ass. "You want to play games mi amore? Okay then" he held my hips up as he repeatedly connected his into mine making me cry out to into the air. "Let's play them" his lips attached my nipple.

When I looked down Enzo sent me a week as he marked all over my chest with his lips, a hand still on my throat, Enzo thrusted faster until his name was the only one my brain could remember. "I've been getting tired of this mouth of yours Violette, maybe I should put it better use, but as the little slut that you are you would love that."

I could only manage a whimper. "Fuck" he said as I pulsed around him. "This perfect fucking body, these beautiful lips, you Violette Luna Bianchi are mine."

"Mine to fuck" he said between thrust. "Mine to use like a little slut" and most in importantly he slammed his hips up one more time before we came. He held my face in his hands as I came down from my high. He pushed the curls from my face looking between the both of my eyes.

"Mine to love forever and more"

"Damien, the next time you send me on one of your pathetic drug trades at least make them interesting" I said through the mic.

The sound started breaking off when I tossed the piece of shit in the garbage. I whistled a tune in my head walking deeper down the hallway.

The sound of water falling from the roof slowly dripping into a puddle was starting to annoy the crap out of me. I just wanted someone's blood on my knife tonight no matter who's it was.

A gun was cocked behind my head making a grin creep onto my face. I guess dreams really do come true even if they come from sick bastards like myself.

I slowly turned around as his hand quivered in fear, this had to be his first time I almost felt bad.

Almost.

"I'm going to give you five seconds to hand over your gun" Isn't that just cute.

"Five" I rolled my sleeves up to my forearms.

"Four."

"Three" I could finish a whole meal by the time he finishes counting.

"T-Two"

"Come on, surely you know how to count down to one" he could be no less than nineteen.

"On"- I pulled his arm towards me flying my fist at his face hearing his nose crack.

"Fucker, your face almost hurt my hand" I grabbed his gun shoving it in his mouth.

"This isn't how I wanted to spend my night, I got fucked over by someone I cared for and now I'm getting my hands dirty for my bosses brother. Great way to spend my birthday isn't it?" he mumbled something but his gun was to busy being shoved down his throat.

"I can't hear you, you should really speak up."

"Well if it isn't the devil herself" I pulled the trigger turning around to see Angel holding a gun towards my head.

"Come on beautiful, shoot me" I grabbed her hand putting the gun under my chin as I backed her against the wall. "It's no worse then what you've already done to me."

"Mariano I"-

"She asks about you Angel, every fucking night she speaks on how much she misses when you'd read her book. And every night I have to tell her that you went away." her looked away from me but I gripped her chin.

"She cries wanting you to do the little stuff that I can't fucking do with her, when you'd do her hair and make her.. smile. Angel why the fuck did you do it?"

She slowly put the gun down until it fell to the ground. I couldn't help but look over her enticing features, from her memorizing dark skin to her eyes that could fuck me over one hundred times and I'd forgive her no matter what.

Her hand reached to my face as I closed my eyes at missing her touch, it was always there when too soothe my insomnia. She looked between both of my eyes before connecting our lips, her tears fell onto my cheek as it took everything to push away from her.

"I- I can't tell you yet" she tried to reach for me but I backed away, like glass in her eyes it shattered her but she hurt the only person that gave meaning to my life.

"You can hurt me all you want Angel, but the day you're the cause of her tears" I looked down to the bracelet I gave her for her birthday, I scoffed at the face she had the audacity to even wear it.

The bracelet had three charms on it. A knife she picked out to represent me, the rainbow for Iris and the sun for Angel for her smile.

"Is the day you become dead to me." I left her in the dark hall way feeling the anger return to my body.

I drove home gripping the steering wheel until my knuckles turned white.

As soon as I opened the door I was met with two little arms running over to me. "Daddy! I missed you so much" I picked her up as she pressed kisses all over my face.

"How much?" She opened her arms as wide as they can go.

"You missed me to right?" Her little lips curled into a pout. I tickled her stomach until her giggles filled the room, the smile appeared back onto my face.

"O-Okay okay I get it" she caught her breathe. I thanked the babysitter paying her for watching Iris while I was gone.

The bundle of joy grew quiet as she played with my rings. "What's wrong?" I lifted her chubby face into my hands. "Tell me what's wrong little flower"

"The boy at school said no one loves me and that's why mommy and Angel left" her hazel brown eyes started to blur with tears.

Would it be wrong to torture a child?

"I w-want Angel back!" she cried into my neck as her little arms held me tighter. Iris was only nine, she didn't deserve this. I wiped her tears with my thumb pressed a kiss on her forehead.

"What do I tell you every night before you go to sleep?" she messed with her fingers.

She took her small pinky before wrapping it around my much large one. "As long as we have each other" I started.

"I-It's all the love we will ever need" she said before letting out a small yawn. I carried her into her room before letting her curls fall over her pillow. The door bell rung as I removed my shirt from my body.

Angel was looking down at the floor before you to my bare torso then into my eyes.

I was getting ready to shut the door before she stopped it with her hand. "Scream, yell at me curse me out for all I fucking care Mariano. But please don't look at me like I was nothing to you"

"I came to explain... but even if you decide that you don't forgive me Mariano, I won't stop coming back for you because I love you, and I love Iris and you know that." I let her walk in as she sat down but I kept my stance.

"Talk"

how do we like Mariano's POV?

□□□□□□ □□□

"Leonardo and I met when I was seventeen, I worked for him as a maid because he was a family friend. He had been running in and out of the house who would hit on me and make sexual remarks. When he found out that one of his best clients had been trying to harass me, he killed him before he could get any further. Instead of letting me continue as a maid he showed me his part of his life, he taught me how to defend myself and how to... manipulate people."

"I felt like I owed him something but he denied that I didn't until he found about you and Violette.. the card that arrived that time in the cafe, those were his men. He didn't expect you to walk into the jewelry store but when you did that's when he told me to get closer to you." I clenched my jaw.

"For the few weeks I would report back to him about Violette when you introduced me to her. Then when you brought me back here and you didn't expect Iris to be home, I felt like the worst person in the world."

"Time grew into months when I broke the only rule he gave to me and that was not to develop feelings for you. But I couldn't help it Mariano, the way you love your daughter with your whole entire heart, you would burn the world for that little girl"- I cut her off by standing directly in front of her.

Pushing my feelings that threatened to come back for her. "You're right Angel, I would burn the world for her, even if that means I have to burn you in it." she stood up.

"Leonardo found out about us, about Iris. He was at her school that day when I said we ran into car trouble."

"Why the fuck didn't you tell me? Not only did you put yourself in danger but my fucking daughter, Angel I swear to fuck if you let him near her."-

"I would never do that and you know it! I would never put her in danger, that's why I left you because he promised me he wouldn't stop going to her unless I did" I didn't get to respond before the little flower wiped her tired eyes.

"Daddy? You woke me up" I picked her up before apologizing, she held her small giraffe in her hands before turning to Angel.

"Iris"-

"No! you hurt my daddy and me" she said with a quivering lip. She moved from my arms pushing at her legs with her small hands. "I hate you because you left me, I hate you because you made my daddy sad and you made me cry. You promised not to make him sad like my mommy does" The sting in my heart wouldn't go away seeing how my feelings affected her more than it affected me.

I picked her up as she huffed into my arms.

"You should go" I held onto Iris tighter. I wasn't sure if I believed her, part of me wanted to give up and take her back because I could barely sleep without her but the other part of me was thinking for my daughter. If Angel was associated with any parts of Leonardo, I needed her far as possible from Iris.

"I'm sorry to both of you and Violette, I love you both so much please don't forget that." Iris threw her giraffe at the floor her small sniffles in my shoulder as Angel closed the door.

Another knock came to the door as Iris slowly fell asleep in my arms.

"Araceli it's late." I looked at the babysitter seeing what she always does when speaking to me and that's chewing on her lower lip.

"I know sir but I left my jacket" she gestures to the blue coat on the chair. I let her in as she holds her head down to get it, Araceli was a shy girl, she could never look directly into my eyes.

"There was also this outside for you" she hands me a package signed from Violette herself. Didn't think I'd forget your birthday did you?

I chuckle at the package before sitting it on the table. Iris wakes up once again as I apologize but she quickly gets from my arms to Araceli's.

"Ara!!" she screams loudly. "Can you please please please read me a book" she pleads.

"I think it's getting late little flower, we should let her get home."

"No it's okay sir, I'm fine with one story." I agree as she picks her up.

"Araceli" she fixes her fallen glasses.

"Call me Mariano not sir."

I sat on Enzo's lap in a casino, his tattooed tanned hand in between my thighs as the woman in front of the table explains the game.

"Have you ever played before mi amore?" I shake my head as he places a kiss on my shoulder.

"Then you can be my eyes" I nod watching her slip different cards to the different men with cigar's between their lips. She slips an extra one to the guy on the side.

I watch the man on the side of us cockily smile knowing he has the winning card as he waits for everyone to place all their money on the table.

Enzo's thumb caresses my bare thigh as he sees it too. Purposely spilling my drink on him, he shoots up in his seat as everyone's attention turns to him. I quickly switch his card with Enzo's as I try to pretend to be sorry. In doing so I see a woman at the top of the stair case looking down at us.

When she sees me looking up to her she flees behind the curtain.

When he sits down Enzo's lips place a sweet kiss on the side of my neck. "Good girl" he praises making me smile. The fools throw in all their money as the man next to us is confused on how Enzo won.

Enzo tell Alejandro to take the rest of the money as he leads us up the steps. He pulls me into the hall way before connecting our lips. He grips my jaw making me look directly into his blue eyes.

"What I said on the plane Violette, I meant it." I hold his face in my hands as he watches me in lust.

"And I mean when I say this, I love you Enzo" Almost like a thousand emotions flood his perfect eyes as he waste no time to crash our lips together, his teeth sink into my lip drawing a moan from me. His tongue explores my mouth like he doesn't want me to let go. Ever.

I wanted Enzo to paint his kiss all over my body as if I were his canvas, his lips to be the brush, to keep me forever protected. "Say it again" he says in a lower voice this time.

"I, Violette Luna Bianchi love you, Enzo Aleksander Romano."

"How much?" he peppered kisses along my neck, his hand going up my dress to take a handful of my ass. "How much do you love me Violette?"

"Enzo, this is not the time... we have to"- he stopped when I pushed him away from me. He furrowed his eyebrows until he saw the man holding the gun and the bullet connecting with the side of my body.

He quickly reached for his gun before the man could run off he shot him in the back of the head. Enzo caught my body before I hit the floor.

"Don't you fucking dare close your eyes" he said holding the now bleeding bullet wound on the side of my stomach. Tears welled my eyes at the pain, the feeling of Enzo ripping part of his shirt in order to stop the bullet.

"Violette" his words started fade as my eyes started to flutter close. "Fuck, Violette look at me" he lifted me up rushing down the stairs as more pain seized through my side.

"Tesoro please don't close your eyes on me" Alejandro's voice came next as he tried to stop the bleeding but it made things worse.

Enzo held my face in his hands. "I-It's cold.." his thumb swiped over the fallen tear.

"I know tesoro, but I need you to keep your eyes open... for me do it for me." he held my hand as I heard the door to the car shut.

"If you don't drive faster I'm going to fucking kill you Alejandro!" Alejandro sped through traffic, all I could hear was a heart beat picking up, a heart beat that wasn't mine.

"Do you hear that? You have my fucking heart Violette, nobody makes it beat like you do. We're almost there, I love you too fucking much to let our story end like this. Not when we just started." A small tear hit the side of my cheek, it only causes the ones brimming to fall. Enzo hated being vulnerable because he was taught it would get him killed one day, that's why he was so closed off. His emotions were showed to him as a sign of weakness, his heart was caged off before he learned to use it.

"I I can't do this not with out you mi amore, we're going to be okay Violette I promise you. Remember when I said, I know how I wanted my story to end" his voice started to break. "I want it to end with you, with me in your arms forever."

I blinked once then all I could see where white lights and ceilings.

Enzo's voice died out as I heard the beeping of the monitor, my dress being cut open as my eyes closed when a mask was being put to stabilize my breathing.

I would try and hang on.. for him.

there's a book in the making. sadly it's not Mariano's but it is coming soon maybe before this story is complete. I rewritten that book about thirteen times now...

do you think Mariano will take back Angel?

Do you want them back together?

These cliffhangers are becoming a new thing to me.

I was literally going to say the end but decided against it.

□□□□□□ □□□

A soaring pain in my left hip grew. When I looked down, Enzo's heavy arm was thrown over my waist as his fingers were intwined with mine. His head was uncomfortably placed on the side of the bed. I tried to move but he would only hold onto me tighter like he was afraid I would let go.

It's been two days since my surgery, the bullet hadn't hit anywhere fatal it just hurts like a bitch. Enzo refused to leave my side even when the doctor told him about visiting hours.

"Enzo, please move" he groaned shaking his head like a child making me laugh but it caused more pain. When I winced loudly he threw his head up before looking down at me.

"Fuck, I'm sorry" his voice was quiet holding instant regret. His hand fell to my cheek as his thumb caressed it, it closed my eyes falling into his touch. Enzo then ripped his hand away before clearing his throat, I could tell something was wrong with him.

"Enzo" I called out but he was lost in deep thought, placing my hand on top of his he snapped out of whatever he was thinking about.

"I love you" he said placing a kiss to my forehead.

"I love you Enzo, now tell me what's wrong?" he shook his head at the same time Mariano walked in with a little girl who reassembled him.

Her brown hair was braided down her back, she had his brown eyes that resembled the sun along with the light green on the outskirts.

"Gorgeous, I want you to meet Iris" the little girl waved her small hand at me. I held her as Mariano and Enzo walked out to talk. She held out the stuffed giraffe as she giggled when I placed it back in her hands.

When Enzo returned she moved from me straight into his hands as he lifted her into the air then down into his arms.

"Someone tells me you got into a fight at school" she waits for his reaction, when he gives her a small high five it makes Mariano roll his eyes. Mariano then comes to my side pressing a kiss to my forehead and taking my hand.

"She's beautiful Mariano" I say as we watch Iris's face burn red when Enzo tickles her stomach. Her laugh then triggers his own which makes my heart jump at the sight.

"I've never seen him.. smile" He points out Enzo's dimple on his right and left cheek. "I'm not talking about grinning, I mean a genuine smile one that he means."

"He thinks it's his fault you're in here" I scrunch my brows together. That explains why he's been distant since I woke up except for the constant reassurance that he loves me.

"Come on little flower" Mariano takes Iris as she waves us goodbye and they leave Enzo and I alone. When the door shuts I cross my arms when he rubs the nape of his neck. I sigh holding my arms out for him. He sits on the side of the bed instead, I can't help but feel the sting in my heart.

"Enzo, it's not your fault, nothing that has happened to me or us is your fault" I say.

"What are you thinking about?" I start to panic when he stands up running a hand threw his hair. "Enzo talk to me."

"I just.." he turns around taking my hand.

"You're scaring me.."

"I was just thinking, maybe you'd be safer if I sent you away from all of this. From me" he admits making me pull my hand away.

"Maybe you should stop thinking." he sits back down as I try to sit up straighter ignore the slight pain in my hip.

"I'm serious Violette, you wouldn't be in any of this if I hadn't forced you into my life" I'm not sure which one it was but emotions were coursing through me like a tidal wave.

"Forced?" I took a hold of his face, the ping in my heart said other wise when he brushed me off.

"Enzo, you didn't force me into anything. I chose to be more than your dancer, I knew exactly what I was getting into walking into your life"anger began to flow though me.

"I'm just saying, you'd be a lot safer"- I let out a scoff at his words.

"I'm safer with you than away from you Enzo, what if I had never met you and he came looking for me? I would still be living a lie thinking a woman sitting in my home was my mom!" he went silent not even looking at me now.

"If you don't want to be with me Enzo, you can just say that.." My voice began to grow quieter as I crossed my arms across my chest, you get used to people walking out of your life as if you meant nothing to them. But deep down I knew if Enzo left it would leave a deep scar, I felt lump form in my throat at the thought of him leaving.

The small beep of the monitor began to pick up with the speed of my heart beat. "I thought you love me" this made him turn around.

"I'm doing it because I do love you tesoro, so fucking much. I can't have you being hurt not because of me."

"None of this is your fault Enzo, stop blaming yourself for his mistakes, and stop saying your doing this because you love me. If you did you wouldn't be trying to leave me. Stop going through things by yourself when I'm right here."

"It wouldn't be forever, Reid and Adora"-

"Why are you trying so hard to end us?" I was getting tired of trying to prove that I wanted to go through this with him and be there for him. "I've already told you that I'm not going anywhere, but I see that you're so set on leaving me.. then leave Enzo, if that's what you want so fucking bad then just go" his blue eyes were now shut tightly. All of me was hoping he'd just hold me and tell me how stupid he was for ever coming to this conclusion.

"Tesoro you know that's not what I want, I love you too much. I can't have you in danger, they'll always know you're with me if you are" I held the tears in but they were threatening to fall.

"It would be temporary, Reid and Adora have a place far from here. I would visit you anything until this settles over.. mi amore look at me" I kept my eyes on the white wall feeling my heart crack every time he says my name.

I removed the blanket off of me standing up. Ignoring the shooting pain in my hip I pulled him by the coast of his shirt and connected his lips onto mine. "V"-

"You're going to shut up and listen Enzo, I don't know what dumb fucking cell in your brain brought you too this stupid conclusion that in order to keep me safe I had to be away from you, but you need to kill it and tell it that I'm not going anywhere. Don't think for one second that I'm going to leave you so you can go through this by yourself because this involves me just as much as it involves you" Enzo then carefully snaked his arm around my waist pulling me for another kiss.

"Tell me you love me again" he buried his head in the crook of neck.

"I love you Enzo." he placed a kiss to my cheek.

"I know you do mi amore, that's why I'm sorry for doing this" I pulled away but before I knew it a needle was poked into the side of my arm, and my vision grew darker until I couldn't see.

writers block is literally my downfall right now.

▯▯▯▯▯▯ ▯▯▯

Two fucking months since Enzo knocked me out with a needle in my arm. Two months since I've heard or seen him, since I've been living in Italy with Adora and Reid and their children.

No letter.

No call.

Not even a fucking message bird.

Almost as if he's completely left me.

The stitches on my hip now completely healed. I was currently watching Aria make Ace blush harder than I've ever seen a small child blush.

Reid teasing his wife by whispering in her ear making her laugh as he hugged her from the back. I smiled at it all before walking into my room.

Undressing, I stood in the shower letting the steamy water rain down as I twirled his ring on my middle finger, the same ring I saw Enzo wearing during the same night we met. I woke up in bed with it there but the bed was empty.

It would be an understatement to say that I'm pissed at him, I was a mess of emotions.

I wrapped the peach colored towel around my body exiting bathroom, I got dressed for the day heading down the steps. The small patter of the children's feet grew louder as they ran directly past me.

Not expecting the scene in front of me I froze in my tracks. Enzo rose from the seat with a bouquet of different colored flowers that matched each other beautifully, his hair grew longer at the top to the point he had to push it from his face.

Dressed in a black shirt that showed his strong muscular arms and tattoos that I so heavily missed wrapped around me.

Before he could speak, I turned back on my heels going back up the stairs shutting the door. Was I happy to see him? Yes, I could hardly sleep without feeling him next to me but at the same time I was furious at him to the point I wanted to throw the flowers in his stupid handsome face.

"Mi amore open the door" His voice raspier than before.

"I need to hear your voice tesoro please" I clenched my jaw trying not fall into his alluring words.

A few moments of silence behind the door. When I opened it, Enzo forced himself inside. I didn't even get the register anything yet as he lifted me up into his arms connecting his lips onto mine, the first instinct was to run my hands into his soft hair.

The familiar taste of cinnamon fell off of his lips onto mine, he shut the door with his foot laying me flat on my back on the bed. He groaned into my mouth when I harshly bit into his lips before pushing him off of me.

"You don't get to go MIA for two months and come back as if nothing happened" My chest was still rising and falling all together staring at his now swollen lips.

Enzo's eyes were still fallen dark at my chest. "I'm sorry Violette" I scoffed.

"The last time you said that I ended up waking up in someone else's home, I'm still so fucking mad at you Enzo" his face softened stepping towards me when I climbed up the bed to rest on the head board.

"I know you are tesoro, but you have to understand I didn't do it because I wanted to. Hell I couldn't even fucking close my eyes without seeing your beautiful smile and feeling bad for that day" he leaned over me holding himself up with one hand on the head board using the other hand to turn my chin to him.

"Do you still love me?"

"I will always love you Enzo, I just can't bare to look at you right now" For two reasons, I'm being stubborn and because I want nothing more than to fuck you but this isn't our house.

The door opened and I took the opportunity to push Enzo off me. Ivan the new guard that has been going every where with me entered. He first blushed when he saw me then cleared his throat when he saw Enzo.

"Is there something you needed?" Enzo said rudely next to me. I rolled my eyes standing up, taking the bowl of strawberries from Ivan I thanked him kindly only making him blush further.

"Thank you" he nodded before rushing out, the door shut closed in my face. I turned to see a very jealous Enzo as I took an innocent bite of the strawberry looking up at him.

I held one to his lips. "Want one?" he said nothing. "I guess not"

"Is that why you can't stand to see me right now?" I creased my eyebrows together until I realized what he meant.

"You think I've been fucking him?"

"Yes Enzo, I fucked him" I said with my voice laced in sarcasm. His hand came around my neck closing the space between us. He lifted my hand in the air the one with his ring before placing a kiss to my knuckles.

"I don't think you have mi amore" he cockily rose his thick eye brow.

"How would you know? You haven't been here for two months" he snuck his hand between my parted thighs up my dress. He cupped my pussy in his hands as I cursed myself from growing wet just at the sigh of him.

Pushing my curls from my ear he used his teeth to graze my ear lobe. "Because he's not me Violette, no one knows how to make you cum, or how to beg them to stop better than I do" his lips pressed softly to my neck before his tongue laid flat on my vein marking the spot causing me to close my eyes and bit my lip morning giving him the satisfaction of the noise he wants to hear.

He pushed my thong out of the way coating his finger in my arousal. Sitting the bowl on the side of the table, Enzo pushed one finger into me before placing the finger into his mouth. "You know what I missed so much?" I couldn't respond feeling my eyes flutter close.

"I've missed these lips" he tugged my bottom lip down. "How good you looked with my marks all over this neck" he ran a thumb over the fresh mark making me shiver in pleasure. Entering two of his fingers in me I moaned feeling my walls clench around him.

"How good you feel when you clench around my fingers and how good you take my dick inside of you" he curled his fingers at the right spot to make me release a moan into his neck.

"The sound of your voice when you say my name, hearing the beat of your heart when you let me sleep on your chest. God I've missed you so bad"he smashed his lips onto mine, he pumped his fingers faster until I couldn't hold back anymore and released on his fingers.

I finally caught my breathe when he pulled away, I didn't want to make it that easy for him. I held his face in my hands barely touching his lips, his hard was pressing on my thigh when he groaned as my knee ran up his leg.

"If you think that was going to help you Enzo" I pressed a soft kiss to his jaw. "You are clearly mistaken" he looked confused with I opened the door. Truth was I was close to breaking but I wanted to stubborn a little bit more.

"Surely you didn't believe you were going to sleep in the same bed as me" he clenched his jaw. He was going to tell me everything tomorrow because I needed answers.

"Good night Enzo"

obviously having two books published isn't for me so I'm going to wait until this is fully completed.

I hate how short my chapters are becoming.

I want to start an instagram account to update you guys on my books & update schedules & future book ideas.

□□□□□□ □□□

Two Months Ago.

"I'm going to take a wild guess and say she didn't agree the first time" He ran a hand down his face.

"She's a stubborn woman and I love her for it" he pushed her curl from her face.

"When do you plan on leaving?" he said not looking at me but at the beauty resting in front of us.

"Not until you get your happy ending."

"I've already found my happy ending Mariano, question is when will you find yours?"

"There's not a happy ending for all of us" I muttered under my breath.

Enzo was lucky to have someone like Violette, I would be lying if I say I didn't at first find her attractive at first sight until I saw how spent she was over him.

Raising Iris was something I've done since she was born, seeing her mother leave for another man was hard at first until I realized all the love I needed was in my daughter.

"I'm going for a smoke" I sighed leaving the hospital. Standing in front I brought the cigarette to my lips letting the grey cloud of smoke washed away by the wind.

I wanted more for her than to see this life, she wanted to see the world. Visit different places and try different things, I would do anything for her even if that meant leaving this life behind so she could be happy.

Her happiness meant more than me than my own.

I stepped on the cigarette putting it out before returning to Enzo. They were already pushing the cart with Violette out the back into the car. "She's going to kill you when she wakes up" he chuckled knowing it was true.

"They need to believe that's she's gone" I nodded entering the hospital again sneaking in the doors where the keep all the files.

Searching around with the tint flashlight in my mouth I looked for her name.

"Can I help you?" A sultry voice spoke. I turned to the door which shut.

I guess this day isn't totally shit.

The doctor standing in front of me, well she was fucking breath taking. Black curls pulled into a bun with some falling from the top to the sides, her lips were full covered in gloss. She wore black glasses framing her brown eyes that could make someone fall to their knees.

Covered in a coat was her curvy body but the white top didn't stop her breast from poking out. Her skin was rich and smooth, brown resembling Violette's.

"You're not supposed to be back here" she crossed her arms fixing her glasses first. Her name tag read Grace Pierce, smart and sexy.

Just my fucking type.

She took the file from my hands. "This is doesn't belong to you" I didn't have time for this, though I wanted to stay and hear her voice. I needed to go.

"Let's make this easier for both of us shall we beautiful" she backed into the door as I stepped closer.

Taking the file from her hands she reached for it but instead I placed her hand above her head.

"As much as I would love to stay, I can't. Now I'm going to need you to forget you ever saw this."

"You mean witnessing you breaking several federal laws?" she tilted her head. I snuck my index finger under her chin making her brown eyes look up into my green ones not missing the way they traveled over my freckles.

"Exactly, though it may be hard for you to forget such a handsome face" she covered her laughter with a scoff.

"You're full of yourself."

"I could be full of something, but I don't kiss on the first date."

"This isn't a date, I don't date criminals, I like nice guys" I held a hand to my heart.

"I'm sure you do, you go for the nice guys right? The ones that'll buy you flowers only and drop you off home and go on about their day. But me, I would get you flowers, then fuck you into the next morning." Her brown eyes widened, I leaned in closer to take in the scent of coconut and vanilla.

"There's nothing nice nor slow about me Grace, I prefer rough and fast until you can't even remember your own name." I took the file back from her hands opening the door.

"See you around beautiful" I shut the door grinning to myself at her awe struck expression.

Present

"Iris you have to pick one" I watched my nine year old daughter stand in the ice-cream shop with her hand on her chin thinking hard between strawberry and chocolate chip ice-cream.

"But it's hard, there are so many" she exclaimed making her brown curls jump off her shoulders.

I lifted her into my arms. "How about I get you both on two separate cones?" she nodded her head happily as the man behind the counter handed her two cones.

I was going to regret this when she can't go to sleep tonight.

"Today's all about you little flower" I walk us out of the small shop while her face is a mess of pink and chocolate ice cream around her lips.

She holds the strawberry cone to my lips and giggles softly when she pushes it against my lips.

I take out the napkin cleaning her mouth but she continues to lick the treat making more of a mess. I set her in the car making sure her seatbelt is secured before driving to the hospital.

"Am I sick daddy?" She finishes the last of her small cones cleaning her hands.

"It's just a small fever" She lays her head in the crook of my neck as I carry her through the familiar surrounding.

The nurse ask me to wait in the room for the doctor, it may have been a small fever but I was on the verge of freaking out. Iris was the one person I had to help my insomnia, sleep ness night she'd crawl underneath the blanket and ask me to read to her and attempt to read to me.

Iris looked a mix of me and her mother, she had my brown hair but her curls.

My freckles along with my tanned skin but her button nose that was adorable. This little girl was my world and I couldn't help but feel a purpose in life when she looks at me with her big green eyes.

The door opens, in walks the familiar doctor from two months ago. Grace Pierce.

"Mr. Delrosa" She turns to see me no doubt she recognizes me. "Can I sweetie?" She ask Iris who nods and sits comfortably on my lap.

Taking her temperature I couldn't help but run my eyes over her beautiful features.

The way her eyebrows were perfectly shaped the dimples on both sides of her face, her curls always pushed into a bun now let down freely cascading on her shoulders.

"Everything seems fine" She stood up. "She does have a small fever but nothing serious, she should rest and be put under no stress" Her brown eyes fell onto my hand which was bandage in a white wrap.

"I think I should take a look at that" she reached for my hand.

I stood up before she could keeping Iris close to me.

"Mr. Delrosa, it could get infected" I sat back down placing Iris on the side of me.

She seemed surprise when she dabbed the burning liquid on my hand and I didn't flinch, instead I looked through her glasses to her brown eyes that were avoiding my gaze.

"Still into nice guys?" she gave me a short smile.

"You seem pretty nice to me" By now Iris had her tiny headphones in.

"There's nothing nice about me love" Her eyes meet mine remembering my familiar words.

"You don't seem like a bad person" She would be the first to say that.

"You called me a criminal two months ago" Her angelic laugh filled my ears.

"You stole a patients file Mr. Delrosa."

"Stole, borrowed, took a look at and never returned. Same thing beautiful it was for a good cause" she finished the last of the bandage.

"How did you get this?"

"Better off if you don't know."

"A man of secrets" She stared into my eyes for a while almost like she was trying to figure something out.

"One of many talents as well" The golden silence between us was enough to make me grin.

"Daddy, I'm sleepy" Iris removes her headphones with a small yawn leaning her head on my shoulder.

I thank Grace picking Iris up as she waves her hand at the doctor. "You should come by next week" Grace stops me from leaving the door.

"If it's an excuse to see me again doctor, all you have to do is ask" She rolls her eyes playfully.

"To check her temperature" She points to the small girl in my arms on the verge of falling asleep as I let out a small chuckle.

"Good bye Mr. Delrosa."

if you haven't already you should follow my socials for updates times & sneak peeks of future books!

□ □ □ □ □ □ □ □ □

The view of white snow fell upon the window, I ran a hand through my wet hair. The grey cloud of smoke filled the room, the smell of the cigarette mixed with the dark sky.

I throw my head back closing my eyes only regretting it the moment the memory flashes through out my mind.

"Mama!" I called for her pretending to have hurt my arm, holding it close to my chest, she ran quickly before crouching down to my short height.

With worried eyes, I threw open my arms revealing the white rose. "Happy birthday mama!" I exclaimed making her smile appear, she pulled me into her arms careful not to ruin the delicate flower and it's beautiful petals.

"Grazie mio amore" (Thank you my love). I took her hand opening the large black doors, outside rained snow, my mother's blue eyes widened almost sparkled when she saw the snow.

Her lavender dress blew threw the crazy wind when she ran outside holding my hand. I held the cold snow in my hands before tossing it up in the air for it to rain upon us.

"It's wonderful mama look!" I jumped making prints with my shoes. She fell onto her knees doing the same with her hands as if she couldn't believe it was snowing.

Our first time seeing snow.

She turned on her back holding me close. "You'll get a cold" I scolded her crossing my arms and frowning.

She laughed pinching the bridge of my nose, the white snow fell on her black hair which matched my own. I was happy to see her smiling after hearing her crying the few past days.

Soon the joyful time was ruined when my father pulled me away from her. "August please wait" she called, he didn't listen he reached for something in his pocket. When I saw the gun aimed at me I looked to my mother in fear.

"You or the boy Sofia" She got on her knees pulling at his black shirt. He speaks about me as if I wasn't his son.

"August don't do this, lascialo fuori da tutto questo!" (Leave him out of this)

"I don't have time for this."

He aimed the gun at her this time, I ran in front of it but she pulled my back. "Enzo, look at me" I shut my eyes tightly as she wiped the tears fallen onto my cheek, they felt like ice hitting the ground nothing compared to what my heart was feeling.

"I love you Enzo, I love you so much. Don't ever stop smiling mi amore, your smile is precious too me and it always will be" I shook my head in her hands.

"I don't understand" I felt more tears triggered by the ones that dropped from her eyes, she placed a kiss to my forehead letting it stay there whispering that she was sorry but I didn't know what was happening.

"Forgive me my son" The ring of a bullet passed through ears. My mother gently shoved me out of the way , when I looked down at my body, I was fine. But when I looked at my mother's chest she wasn't.

Her blues eyes that once held love for me closed along with one last whimper of pain from her mouth. I opened my hand to see a silver necklace, the pendant was a heart of the color blue.

"A symbol of our hearts and eyes, which we share" I hear her voice playing in my hands, from the first time she gave it to me for Christmas.

"N-No, mama please open your eyes. Don't close them, open them please" I laid my head on her heart only to hear the beats slow tauntingly until the finally stop. The snow covered her hair, I pushed it away trying to wake her up.

I turned to him, no remorse in his cold eyes. Almost as if they went black, he didn't care.

"I should have killed you instead" he spat leaving me to cry holding my mother's hand, her blood drained into the snow turning it red. I cried out as the coldness took over me, my tears rained on her dress.

"Please you can't leave me mama please!" My voice cracked. Her skin was pale now, her lips parted but no words or air came out.

"I just wanted to make you happy, I just wanted you too see the snow" I looked up to the sky, wondering how such a happy day could go wrong at the hands of the my father.

"Was it my fault? If it was I'm sorry j-just please come back to me" My body fet numb, I didn't care that the snow was causing it because it wasn't just the snow. The only thing I could hear was the sound of a bullet going off repeatedly playing over and over in my head.

"I love you mama" I push the hair from her forehead leaving one last kiss there.

Happy Birthday Mama.

I grabbed the nearest photo frame smashing it against the wall. I didn't want to be here, I didn't want to feel this again not again. The emotions from that day returned all striking at my heart, her face, her smile, him.

They all returned at once, I took the cap off of the amber liquid drowning myself in it until I couldn't feel anything, I wanted to feel numb. Pulling at my hair, I shut the curtains, I didn't want to be reminded but it all just wouldn't stop playing in my head over and over.

"You killed her!" I scream at him, my finger tips began to feel numb laying in the snow.

"She chose to be killed Aleksander, she chose your life over yours. Quite frankly I'm not sure why, you're a pathetic excuse of a son."

He pulls me up by my shirt. "One day you'll learn what it means to be a real man, you're a monster at heart Aleksander just like me, you can never be loved."

"I will never be like you" I refuse to believe his words.

Every day since then, I couldn't understand why she would chose me over her or why he felt the need to kill her.

Maybe I was like him, I killed with no remorse but never to be loved, that's where he was wrong.

I clutch the chain in my hands only downing the liquid ignoring the burning taste.

When it's empty, a soft knock comes to my door. Violette's soft voice comes from behind it, I can't let her see my like this.

I stand in the bathroom mirror, my eyes were bloodshot red, my hair falling over my face until I moved it out of my way. "Enzo, are you okay?" her voiced laced in worry when she opens the door. I can't but help but remember hear the sound of the gun going of off.

Violette's hands hold my face as she moves my hair seeing how bad my condition is. "Tesoro" my voice breaks, she pulls me into her arms letting my cry in her neck, I let my hands hold her tightly afraid that she'll just disappear but like every one else.

She's the only person I have left, I can't afford to lose her. I just want to disappear in those brown eyes, take her away from this some where quiet and peaceful just for us.

After awhile she runs a warm shower, the feeling of my heart began to break thinking that she was leaving but she removed her dress stepping in with me. I let her wash my hair until she just let me hug her letting the emotions be whisked away by the sound of her breathing.

"Help me forget Violette, I don't want to feel like this anymore" she lifted my head, her own tears started to fall before she let her lips gently press down on mine.

"I'm here Enzo" Her thumb stroked my cheek as she gives me her best smile.

"That's all I need" I say turning off the water, drying her body, the beauty in front of me begins to worry again seeing that I'm still drunk. "You're all I'll ever need"

She carefully lets me lay in the now cold sheets covering my lower half which is still in a towel. Panicking again when she reaches to turn off the light and leave, I grab her wrist softly.

"Stay with me.. please" her brown eyes saddened, she turned off the lamp climbing in the bed next to me, her body was always so warm, her scent was addicting. Her arms wrapping around me as mine did around her waist made the beat of my heart calm just by holding her.

"I love you so much tesoro" I say laying my head on her chest. I hold the pendant around my neck.

"And I love you Enzo" I close my eyes to the sound of her voice.

She let her fingers run in my hair telling me that she loves me again and it would get better. "Promise me" she stopped but I tapped her thigh for her to continue which she did.

"Promise me you won't lose me to the chaos." I wanted Violette for the rest of my life, I wanted her touch, her lips, her body, her heart, her mind forever.

"I promise Enzo."

Chapter Thoughts?

* Not Edited Yet *

□ □ □ □ □ □ □ □

For the past week I haven't slept a full night, the want to end Leonardo's life was growing every minute. I couldn't close my eyes until I felt Violette hands run and mess threw my hair.

The sound of water dripping from the pipes to the hard smell of cigarettes irritated me further.

Leonardo killed Henry, his body popped up somewhere in a lake close to the hotel he was laying to rest at, smart man. It's faster to hide and run without worrying about someone slowing you down. I puffed the cigar smoke from my lips into the air, handing it Mariano he repeated the steps.

When we got into the door we Mariano froze and I just rose an eyebrow.

Angel was tied up with her head thrown down, a knife in her thigh and clean shot to her neck. Mariano clenched his jaw not bothering too look in front of him. "I guess he's killing loose ends"

"He's scared is what he is, he believes I killed his daughter without remorse now he's killing anyone that could help us too him" I turned to Mariano.

"She's not important too you?" he looked at Angel's now dead body back to me.

"Not anymore" I nodded allowing us to leave her body there too rot.

I just wanted to go home and see the one smile that could make my heart go from ice to a melting puddle, I wanted to be in her arms, feel her touch and have her love.

"What's that?" Mariano pointed to the small black box I pulled out of my pocket.

I quickly stuffed it into my pocket. "Nothing" I replied clenching my jaw and looking out the window.

Mariano stopped me when I got out the car. "Dirà di sì" (She'll say yes) I didn't respond.

Instead I opened the door letting a hand fix the mess of hair on my head. Food was already on the table with a small note from my angel upstairs telling me that she couldn't wait for me because she got too hungry with an apology and a sad face.

I laughed quietly, I know she loves me, so why was I so fucking afraid of her saying no and shattering my heart like non-important glass?

I opened the bedroom door, the sight alone was enough to make me smile.

Violette had a pen in her mouth and a book in her hands, her smooth freshly shaven legs bent up holding the book in it's place.

The white silk robe clung to her body, she looked up when I began to remove my pants. Her eyes trailed all over my tattoos covering hidden scars, down to my erection and she laughed.

The sound like music to my ears.

"I cooked just in case you got hungry" she carelessly flipped through her book. She watched me with careful eyes as I got onto the bed slowly, she warned me by calling out my name but the way she just pressed her thighs together I know she wanted it too.

"Shh tesoro, let me make you feel good hm?" I spread open her soft thighs, letting my lips place burning flames to her brown skin. Her book was long gone along with the page she was on, I softly bit on the skin marking it as mine.

"Please don't tease me Enzo" My angel breathlessly said but I wanted to take this slow.

"Patience tesoro" she whined before complying, I kissed the inside of her other thigh. Her arousal was only growing at my slow and teasing pace.

I pushed up the white silk on her body revealing her glistening pussy not covered by anything. I let my finger collect her wetness before she grabbed it and placed them in her mouth.

Her eyes fluttered close when my mouth enclosed where she wanted me, she moaned around my fingers still tasting her sweetness. I don't think I could ever get over how fucking good she tasted.

She kept her lips on my fingers like my good girl, I sped up the pace using my tongue to lap over her clit which only brought more pleasure to the beautiful goddess who was watching me with those honey brown eyes.

The softness in them made my heart bloom open like a flower in spring. She brought me feelings, I was taught not to have.

I gripped her hips lapping my tongue faster making her arch her back, her hard nipples poking through the white silk as she used her hand to grasp her breast. "I love you" she called out, she kept whispering the words into the air nearing closer to her release.

What ever pain I had gone through in the past was wiped away just by her words. Words people would call simple and reassuring but coming from Violette they were the words I had been dying to hear after mother died.

The woman in front of me coming on my tongue was the one I wanted forever, she had my heart in her hands since I laid eyes on her dancing on a pole. She kissed my bruises and washed away the dried tears painted on my skin.

"Enzo" I closed my eyes at the sound of her sultry voice saying my name, the only one who could make my name matter was her, the sound of it was soft and fell off like the silk on her body.

She came again trying to close her legs but I was far from making her feel good.

Her moans were heavenly, I let her nails dig into my shoulders as she created a pain that fell into an enjoyable pleasure. I would let her taint her kisses all over my skin because my body was her canvas, she was the painter and her lips, her tongue, her nails. Everything about her was the paint.

When she came for the last time she panted heavily, I used my fist on either side of her to hold myself up staring down at her flustered state. I pushed the curl from her beautiful face, the face I wanted to wake up too every morning.

"You are beautiful mi amore" She bit on her lip dropping her gaze to healed bullet on her hip. It was a now bright white line contrasting with her delicate skin.

I held her cheeks in my hands making her look at me. "You. Violette Luna Romano. Are Beautiful. Your scars are beautiful. And I love you more than you can ever imagine" I said in between pecks to her soft lips. "Sì?"

"Yes, Enzo" I saw the light in her eyes beam when I used my last name instead of her own.

"Mhm, I need too hear you say it" her big doe brown eyes stared into mine, her arms wrapped around my neck pulling me closer.

"You. Enzo Aleksander Romano. Are beautiful" I laughed along with her, placing my tip at her entrance. I slowly pushed into her, though she was already used to how big I was.

I didn't want to fuck her hard.

I didn't want to fuck her quick and have this moment be over.

I wanted to make love to her and feel her closer than ever. No matter how deep I pushed in, it felt like I wasn't close enough. Her soft moans filled my ears, her nails clawing down my back while my head was buried in the mess of beautiful black curls sprawled over the pillow.

I lifted her leg to the side of my hip, she noticed that I was making love to her at the slow pace. I leaned down to suck on her neck, wanting the world to know that she was mine, I left my love bites on her chest and on her neck. Her sounds being heard throughout the crisp night.

She held my face in her hands, she kissed my lips deeply, both of our moans being transferred onto each other's lips. Then she began to paint my skin with her lips, down my jaw, to my neck. I kept my pace until picking up my pace.

Cursing into the air when her warm tongue ran over my vein to the mark now on my skin. "Fuck I love you so much" she closed her eyes but I held my hand down on her throat.

"Look at me Violette, let me see those pretty eyes" she complied, her lips parting open.

She cried into the night, as she pulsed around me. She held back wanting to come with me, I watched her twist her nipples with her fingers making the scene in front of me unspeakably captivating.

The sight alone, of her curls all over the pillows, her now swollen red lips opened. The sound of her moans to the red marks on her skin.

This woman could break my heart and I'd still be so deeply in love for her. She could stab a knife directly in my heart and I would still want to be in her arms. "Enzo I'm coming" she broke me out of my thoughts.

"I know tesoro, come for me. come with me" I pulled out and slammed into her hitting her spot making her back arch as she came around me, my head was thrown back as I cussed loudly breaking any silence in the night sky.

In the beginning I believed that I couldn't be loved because of the scars on my heart, that someone so perfect could never think past about all the bad that I've done in my life.

People like me didn't deserve someone like Violette, she didn't deserve the heartbreak that came along with me but both of us were far from letting go.

Chapter thoughts?

I'm debating how I should end this story.

* not edited*

□□□□□□ □□□

The rain calmed me, something about each droplet like ice hitting against my skin. I couldn't help but fall into my own pit of darkness, I left Iris with Violette. Not wanting her too see what her father used to be.

I was seven when my mom started drugs, dad had finally had enough of her shit to the point he remarried and started a new family forgetting that his sons even existed.

She'd send me at the latest nights to get her drugs, the man across the street with his wife who constantly smoked and blew it my face, made it feel like my lungs were closing as if someone were strangling me.

Every night I handed her a bag of drugs, every night I came home with a new knife scar on my side.

I used ice packs to numb the pain that couldn't seem to go away but the pain wasn't hidden in the scar, it was hidden in my heart.

I felt like I didn't matter to anyone and that I would never have anyone. I hated myself for things that were her fault, seeing my dad hold another son like his own only brought more suffering.

I wouldn't eat for weeks which triggered my eating disorder, insomnia to where I couldn't sleep without waking up in cold sweat and screaming out in pain at the memory of being held down why the woman craved her knife into me.

I felt worthless like trash everyone ignores on the street and kicks around until it's no more.

Until Emilio came along.

I remember feeling like a kid in the candy store, the thought of being an older brother excited me and scared me because I didn't know how to be a protector of someone if I couldn't protect myself.

Because of all the drug intake, Emilio came out with a hard stutter. He didn't learn how to speak until he was five but that didn't stop me from making sure I was always there for him.

She wanted to send him too fetch the drugs and I wouldn't let her, we yelled throughout the house until she finally passed out.

He was in the corner with his hands on his ears and his knees tucked close to him. "M-Mariano, i-is everything o-okay" when I saw him cry it was like a million pieces of sharp glass had pierced through my heart at once.

Emilio couldn't sleep not unless I was next to him, I made sure to hold him tight and read one of the books I had saved money to buy for him.

The book was about two birds who were brother's, the oldest was the blue bird and the youngest was the red.

I had turned seventeen, I gotten a job so I couldn't have been home much to be with him which both broke my heart and struck fear.

I kept my door locked, food and water with the key too my bathroom and the two pills if started to panic again.

I had been saving up for the both of us, he told me how he wanted to go to Paris and I promised that I would take him some day.

My boss was an asshole who hated me, he made me stay overtime sometimes even after everyone's left.

I ran home that night faster than my legs could go, a burning pain shot through them but I needed to get back to him before his panic attacks happened. I left him two pills and water bottles if they did and I wasn't there.

I was too late, yelling and screaming came from the apartment. Emilio's voice screaming at her for the way she used all the money I saved up for us to buy drugs, I haven't ever heard him talk so clearly before.

I opened the door to see Emilio on the floor with his cheek with a small cut, drugs spilled on the floor and she stood over him with a knife in her hands.

I acted fast before she could stab him, I pulled his arm and the blade jammed in my back.

Nothing was clear after that, she hit her nerve that struck my body of all it's movements —she gasped in horror after what she had done until she said the final words before fleeing. "That'll teach the pathetic boy a lesson" then the door slammed.

Emilio's cries we're all all that I could hear, the sound of loud sirens and neighboring voices.

My cheek was being patted by a woman who was also praying for me to wake up.

Daisy.

The woman who lived upstairs, the one who would take me into her home giving me actual clothes and food.

My vision was nothing nothing more than a blur but I could see her clearly.

Big black curls that she never once removed out of it's crazy style. Brown eyes which held a kind heart and warmness of summer. Daisy, her name was just a reflection of summertime, soft, calm and bright.

"Come on sweetie you're going to be just fine" I felt her hold my hand and the sound of Emilio begging me to open my eyes.

The sirens hurt my ears and I begin to panic, I want to yell out make it stop but the words were trapped in my throat like a ball. My body began to unsteadily shake, flashes of knives and the woman's face and her husbands almost as if they were reaching out to me to hurt me again.

Please don't let them get to. My younger voice says.

"Please safe him, he's all I have" I hear Emilio's voice before the light around me dies into a pit of black.

The next morning Daisy snuck me out of the hospital with Emilio after hearing police speaking about giving him to a foster home.

We packed all his things setting them in the car.

I almost slipped away from him once and I wasn't going to have to live with the fact that maybe he was going through all the pain again.

"I- I love you M-Mariano" Emilio places a kiss at my cheek with a quivering lip.

"Not as much as I love you" I take off the silver chain on my neck clipping it around his.

"Never take it off, I'll find you again and I expect you too be wearing it sì?" he nods with his big green eyes filled with tears reminding me of a rainforest.

"I will never ever take it off" I can't help but smile when he doesn't stutter. "Promise to find me again so we can go to paris" he holds up his tiny pinky finger and I can't help but hear my voice crack with my next words.

I take out book with the two birds handing it to him before connecting our pinkies. "I promise you little buddy, I'll never stop until I find you"

"I'll read this when I miss you" his small lips turns into a frown and he throws his short arms around my neck crying into my shoulder.

"You're going to be reading a lot then" he sadly laughs and I hold him tightly messing with his brown hair.

"We have too go now Mariano" Daisy wipes her own tears but I neither of us can let go.

"You take care of him Daisy, please take care of him" I place him in the car and he refuses to let go.

"I will with my whole heart Mariano" I looked at the both for the last time before that car drove off.

Merry Christmas Emilio.

I hold the note Angel sent to me a few days ago but I've been too much of a dick to open it.

I take out the knife cutting it open. Her dried tears stain the dirty white paper.

Dear Mariano.

Maybe you'll decided to forgive me in a few months or years. Or maybe never, and I'm okay with that, I feel like crap for what I did and I can't take away the pain that I caused but I can at least explain it.

Never once did I lie about the words I said too you or Iris, both of you grow continuously in my heart even now that I'm writing this.

Other than feeling as if I owed my whole life to Leonardo, you showed me a world that wasn't just painted in black and white but in different colors until you helped me paint myself back into the person I was before he kidnapped me.

If you're looking for me it's too late, Leonardo has already found out that I betrayed him and has probably gone into hiding.

But it's never too late for me to tell you how much I love you and Iris, a freckled smile that had fucked over my plan since I saw you in the jewelry store.

It hurt me so damn much when you got shot to the point I hated myself, I wanted to take that bullet from you and put it in my heart.

You deserve better, someone who looks at you with kindness at first sight not forced.

Who ever they are who comes along Mariano, I hope they show the love that you truly deserve.

Because if it's anyone who deserves the entire world Mariano, it's you and the little girl who you care oh so much about.

With that I want to say that I'm sorry, and I hope you can forgive me for everything.

- Angel.

I throw my head back on my bench, the rain grew heavier and the knife in my hand resting on my palm. I remove the silver ring from my pinky.

The blue and red bird tattooed right on it.

Slower and slower someone was dying because they loved me, either they died or got hurt. I couldn't help but blame myself, I was a train wreck since birth and I couldn't do anything about it.

I forgave Angel a while back, I know what it felt like to think you owe someone your whole life because they help you with the heart ache.

I met Iris's mother in the same way, told me she would help and she did until she reopened scars that I tried so hard to close. Day's she would do nothing but tear them open again and make them deeper, I wanted to leave until she told me she was pregnant.

The hospital had said she requested to leave without letting me know. I didn't know how to be a father, I was ready to give it all up.

Then Iris tugged on my pinky finger, when I looked down at her. She smiled at used my finger to push her nose and she giggled.

I realized not only did I have to learn how to fend for myself but I already had the experience of taking care of someone, I was forced to grow up before I could ever celebrate one of my birthday's.

Then I found Enzo Romano, I don't know what it was but when he looked at me then at the child in my hands he opened his car door I knew I found the person I truly owed my life too.

Where he found Violette, the light to everyone's life and the light to mine.

Mother was found dead from an overdose two weeks after I sent Emilio away and my dad well he's still living life with his family.

I folded the note into a small swan, placing it in the puddled river I let the rain and wind cast it out into the world.

"Daddy!" My little girl screams running into my arms with two big presents. "I missed you so so much" I kiss all over her small face.

"Have you been crying daddy?, don't be sad" she pouts and I can't help but think of Emilio.

"I'm okay little flower, don't worry about me. Did you like your presents?" she jumped up and down holding up the snow globe.

"I love it, it's so pretty" I lift her up tickling her stomach. She shakes it excitedly watching the snow fall all around the small orb.

"Just like you" she thanks me before handing me a long black box.

"This came from you" I look to Adora and she shrugs while her children fight over toys.

I open it seeing my necklace with a note on top. "He's waited long enough, come see him."

Emilio was older now, way fucking older. He was a teenage now holding the present I sent him, I made sure to send him one every holiday and birthday so he knows I'm still here.

He smiles at the camera and holding a book I haven't been able to see in years. "I've memorized all the words now, I miss you a lot" the card is signed and I can't help but build tears in my eyes.

"Daddy? Who is it from" I look at my daughter in front of me. I hug her tightly and she giggles in my ear, that laugh has gotten me through years that I've spent wanting to give up. Her hair smells like bubblegum, the new soap she's been obsessing over recently and it makes me laugh.

The image of Emilio and Iris kept me going and not being a shitty father or older brother. For the rest of my life they would be the only one's that mattered, I was going to find him and introduce them and take them to Paris.

They reminded me of so much of each other, wanting to travel the world. The stutter when they were first born. They shared something with each other, their care for me was all I could ever want in the world.

But then I see Daisy and squint my eyes, she looks so familiar and I can't figure it out until Violette walks into the room.

I turn the card over to find her signature. Daisy Luna Perkins to Mariano DelRosa.

Fuck.

Chapter thoughts?

I cried writing this and I'm just going to go to sleep, I practically broke my own heart.

* not edited might be mistakes*

I might go back and rewrite it, what do you think?

□□□□□□ □□□

I can't help but panic at the photo, she was a spitting image of me. The big curls, the brown skin we heavenly shared, the big doe brown eyes that enlightened in any room.

"Mariano, I don't know if I can do this" I say turning to him, my heart practically punching it's way out of chest.

Mariano turned to me holding Iris who was sleeping in his neck. "You've got this gorgeous, if you want to leave at anytime tell me okay?" I nodded and he held his hand out for me.

We boarded Enzo's private jet and I looked back at the handsome man yelling into his phone. Those captivating blue eyes lift to look at me, he throws me a wink and I smile waving him off.

I get ready to take a step but my arm is being pulled and I'm falling into his warm embrace. He connects our lips softly and deeply, his lips intoxicating me.

Mariano was going to see his brother and I was going to meet my mother.

Enzo couldn't go because he had to make sure he finds Leonardo. I understood because I didn't know how this meeting would go.

What if she doesn't like me?

What happens when she looks at me and doesn't recognize me or worse she doesn't want to see me?

"I'll be waiting for you mi amore" he placed a loving kiss to my forehead snapping me from my panicked thoughts.

"I love you Enzo" He returned the sweet words helping me up the small stairs, not before grabbing a handful of my ass.

I smacked his hand away making him laugh, I kissed his lips once more before the doors closed.

Iris had fallen asleep in Mariano's arms when he read her a book. He was an amazing father no doubt that he was a great brother as well.

"What if she's not my mother just a woman who shares my same face?"

"Whenever you want to leave, I'll be right there."

I nodded before getting comfortable in the seat and dozing off until we made it.

—

Mariano knocked on the door, he was excited too see his little brother but nerves were still kicking my ass.

"Milio, get the door please" We heard a woman's voice, Mariano's hands found mine and gave it a reassuring kiss.

A teenaged boy opened the door before looking at me then Iris who nervously played with her fingers. Then up too a stand talking Mariano, once he saw him, he loudly said his name before hugging him.

Then I finally saw a tear fall from Mariano's eyes as he tightly hugged his brother. "I don't think I can call you buddy anymore, you've grown so much" there were hints of sadness in his eyes.

Emilio was like a twin to Mariano in a teenage boy, the freckled face, green eyes and messy dark hair that was never fixed unless someone did it.

"I- I can't believe you're a-actually here" Emilio didn't dare pull away from his brother, Mariano closed his eyes and let his brother squeeze him almost too death.

"I told you I'd come find you" Just then a woman came from the steps, her eyes found the sweet moment being shared between the brother's.

Then to the small child who was hugging Emilio's leg as if she knew him all her life.

But when she looked to me her smile dropped to one of shock. I felt my heart race pick up, I couldn't help but stare at her as if I couldn't believe that she was real.

Neither of us said a word until Mariano sensed it, "Can we come in?"

"Oh, yes sure please come in" she moved out of the way and I kept my head down walking inside.

Taking a seat on the white couch, she was still in shock too where she bumped into the table knocking over one of the glass cups.

"Crap, I'm sorry" I turned my head away from the broken glass, Mariano let me squeeze his hand not caring if it was too the verge of breaking.

"It's fine, it's just a really loud sound" I bit the inside of my cheek calming my heart rate.

"I can't even begin to wonder what you're thinking about right now."

"For starters, why didn't you take me with you instead of leaving me with a monster?" The words came out harsher than I intended.

She sighed and sat down after cleaning the mess. "I didn't leave because I didn't love you, I didn't leave because I thought of myself. I promise you baby, I tried to take you with me" her eyes began too water.

"You're father was cheater, he constantly put me down even when I was pregnant with you, accused me of cheating and that he would kill me if the baby turned out to be anyone else's. When I was giving birth too you Violette, he was in our home with a random woman missing the chance too see you for the first time" Her words didnt surprise me.

"I remember putting you to sleep, went downstairs because I left your favorite blanket on the couch. Went downstairs for it to see him wiping blood off with it. It was the only thing that could reassure you sleep the full night."

"I had gotten so angry, he was shouting, throwing beer bottles, one of the shards swiped on my cheek when he held it too my face. His sadistic smile appeared because he was proud of it, I heard you crying at the sound of the glass. I went to go get you but he pulled me back and went for you instead."

"He came down the stairs with you in his hands but you cried even when he tried to whistle you too calm down, he handed you too me when you wouldn't stop. Then you finally did, he got so mad he took you back. I asked what he was doing and he said spending time with your child."

"Violette the man didn't even claim you too be his. When I asked why didn't he let me go, he said because he needed you too get what he wanted. I couldn't let him bring you into danger, so I planned too run away" Mariano then put his arm on my shoulder running soothing circles letting me know that he was still here for me.

"When he was asleep, so I thought. I went to your crib, you were gone and so was he. I ran as fast as my lungs and my legs could take me, no one had seen any of you leave until I went back and found him sitting with you in his arms."

"Spending time with your daughter was all he said again, he told me he knew he was leaving but he would dare let me take to with me. He promised if I took you with me he'd find us and not only kill me but you as well, but I did it anyways for the both of us."

"For a year, I believed we were finally safe until I met a man. At the time we had nothing and you were still a crying baby in my arms in need of bed, the man worked for him, lead me straight too him where he sat in a hotel with a gun pointed too my head and you in his arms."

"He told me he wouldn't kill me because he loved me that didn't stop him for taking his anger out on my body, I had seven surgeries due too all the places he fractured. He's the reason I can't have kids now."

"He left me in that hotel room too die, luckily the staff found me and asked me who had done it too me but I didn't say anything because I knew he took you with him."

"Years and years when you were younger, they'd send me your hospital records. From amnesia where he used that to allow you too believe another woman was your mom, to other things that I couldn't forgive myself for" The lump in my throat grew more as she talked, years I felt worthless and hopeless because of it all.

"I moved here wanting to start fresh and find you but it was almost impossible. I thought how could I ever be a mother when I couldn't even protect my actually daughter. Nights I couldn't sleep believing that I had gotten you killed, led me to see a therapist and she told me I needed to let go but I refused." she stood up walking to me.

Her hands held my face as the tears from my eyes hit her palm like a stream. "You can't just give up on your child not even if your heart held not an ounce of hope. I never gave up on finding you. I didn't come up with anything but Violette I need you too know that I tried beyond my power."

"I would have gotten myself killed if that meant I could just see you one more time. I love you with all my heart, and maybe you won't find it in your heart to forgive me but I need you to know. Now that I've found you my sweet Violette."

"I don't plan on missing out of any parts of your life, if you want too get up and leave and never see me again I will be okay because I got too see you today and I will cherish it for all my life" I didn't know how to feel.

I opened my mouth but words were stuck in my throat, I wiped the tears away from her face.

Was it stupid of me to forgive her so easily?

No.

All she's ever done was just for me, I've suffered physically and mentally and so did she.

Every time he hurt me he was hurting her as well, though I got the worse of it.

She was living with the fact that she had gotten her daughter killed and I can't even imagine how pain that felt.

I pressed my forehead on hers. "I just want my mother back, I need you more than ever just be here for me and never leave me again..p -please" my voice broke and she hugged me tightly, she pressed a kiss to my forehead holding me.

"Never again my sweet Violette, never again" I wiped my tears standing up, Mariano had his tears swell in his own in his eyes and he pulled me into his warm embrace, his soothingly rubbed my back before holding my face in his hands.

You gorgeous" he cupped my face. "Are one of the most bravest people I know. Don't even thank me for this because I won't accept it, I would go far and beyond too make you happy."

Mariano believed that he was a broken record, what he didn't know was that he helped people without even realizing it. In many ways he's helped me and I wanted nothing more than to see him happy.

Iris and Emilio sat on the floor while she showed him her stuffed giraffe. "Daddy, can we please go and play video games with uncle Milo" I smiled at her way of pronouncing her name the best she could.

When they went upstairs I turned to my mother. "Who is he?" she pointed to Enzo's ring.

"Words can't explain who is too me mother, all I know is he's the one I want forever" I twisted Enzo's ring around on my finger smiling at the letter R.

"As long as he keeps you smiling like that, I'm all in favor of this man" She took my hand sitting me on the couch.

"We have six hours until our flight, I think we have a lot of catching up too do" Though she was my mother, I know her the I'd like, years cannot be bashed into six hours but I would at least try to get to know the woman I missed out on.

After five in a half long hours of speaking to her, we were both laughing talking memories of her and her amazing friends she was allowed to meet here.

"Tell me about this husband of yours" I laughed shaking my head.

"We aren't married" I cleared my throat.

"After all the things you've just told me about him and all the stuffs he's done for you, he'd be a fool not to marry such a strong woman."

"Ms. D-Daisy, p-please tell Mariano too go back with him" Emilio pouted as did Iris as they came from downstairs.

Mariano sighed knowing if Leonardo was still out there then it wasn't safe for him to know about Emilio or my mother. "How about this" he squatted down to Emilio's height.

"When gorgeous over there get's married, I'll bring you and we can move to Paris just like we've always planned too" his eyes lit up along with Iris's, the two jumped nodding their heads in unison.

"Y-You promise?" Mariano held up a pink with a red and blue bird tattoo and Emilio's lip began to quiver when he took it.

"Promise" Iris's short finger barely fit around theirs.

"I promise too!" she jumped.

I just wanted too get home and be in his arms again, the thought of Enzo proposing crossed my mind the whole plane ride back.

chapter thoughts?

new book coming in one day!

opinions about any character?

we're inching close to the end!

* not edited might have mistakes*

□□□□□□ □□□

The sleeping beauty lies on my chest slightly awake while I let the tips of my fingers gently brush over her arm. Her legs tangled in with my own, her head lying directly over my heartbeat. Her brown eyes drowned like honey flutter open, I felt her soft lips gently press over my heart.

She leans up pressing more kisses around my inked sin cherishing each scar, each heart ache and break. I can't help feeling my heart beat faster with her touch. Each kiss was like heaven; they only brought me life.

She straddles my lap looking down at me tracing each ridge of my abs and muscles. "Happy birthday Enzo" she finally says. I try to reach out for her when she climbs off my lap but fail when she skips over to a black box with a golden bow on it.

I sit up against the headboard and she places it in my lap. "I hope you like it" she nervously bites her lip watching me untie the knot.

Inside the box is a painting, the painting shows my mother holding me as a child. "Mariano painted it for me, and I found the photo in that closed off room you.. I'm sorry if it was an invasion of privacy but I just wanted to give you something"-

I cut her off with a kiss on her lips, I pulled her onto the bed making her straddle me once more. "It's perfect, you're perfect. I love you Violette" I can't help but let a tear fall past my eyes looking at the painting, for years I haven't been able to look at a photo of her, not once.

She would have loved Violette.

She sits between my legs with her back pressed against my chest smiling down at the painting. "I was four in this photo. She brought me my first camera and I couldn't put it down to save my life. I took photos of everything, her, myself, little things that made her smile. When she died in my arms, I believed that I wasn't going to be happy ever again. That all people would see me as a broken man who was broken since he was a child" I turned her face to me so I could stroke her cheeks.

"But you aren't Enzo" her thumb softly strokes over my hand tattoo. "You saw your mother die in your arms, no child or adult should ever see that at such a young age. You have a good heart it's just been through so much" she then traced her name over my heart, I closed my eyes just feeling the moment in her arms.

I want this woman for the rest of my life, every part of her, every breathe she takes. All the times she'd ignore me for small things, her laugh, her kind heart. Her addicting lips to each beautiful stretch mark she had on her hips. I wanted all of it for the rest of my life and yet I didn't know how to say the three words.

Simple is what someone would call them.

Saying them to Violette would be more than just simple, I wanted them to be special. Words she'd go to sleep hearing and smiling when she thought of them.

"Enzo?" I hummed in response. "We're going to be okay right?" she turned around gently placing the beautiful present onto the side of me.

"When this is all over, what are we going to do?" she turns on her stomach, leaning her chin on my stomach.

I stroke her cheek and she leans into my touch, I watch her brown eyes swirl in many ideas. "Whatever you want to do mi amor, I'll be right there" she smiled brightly.

She gets up holding her hand out for me. "Today isn't about me but you Enzo" I take her hand as she leads me to the bathroom, she turns on the luxurious large shower.

I lean against the door frame while her back is turned to me, the black silk on her body slowly falls off revealing all her beautiful curves.

"Care to join me Mr. Romano" she walks over to me, her hands tug at the waistband of my sweats. I remove them kicking them to the side

"Always Mrs. Romano" she bits her lip at my words, we step into the warm water falling over our skin. I stand with my back facing the water so it doesn't hit her instead it pours down my back.

Somehow her lips always taste so addicting, a strawberry taste lingers on her tongue. My hands roam around finding the globes of her ass, squeezing hard as she moans into my mouth.

She begins to place burning kisses down my neck to my jaw, her tongue pressing flat on my skin until she marks the area and claims it as hers.

I'd let her mark my entire body without a single complaint, the world needed to know that I was hers.

She tugs my hair to the side harshly knowing how much I enjoy the pain of it.

I go to run my fingers up her thigh but she stops me, she gets on her knees instead. Looking up at me with those mesmerizing eyes, she pumps me in her hand and I can't help but let my lips part.

Her soft lips wrap around my tip, she pushes her head down enough to take all of me and I curse loudly holding onto her hair. She looks so fucking good with my dick in her mouth, her tongue runs up my veiny shaft up to my tip where she lightly runs her tongue around it making me bit hard on my lip.

"It's your birthday, use me for your pleasure" she says, letting me hold her head down until she begins to gag, relaxing her throat. Tears begin to fill her pretty eyes as she looks up to me. I feel myself touch the back of her throat and I can't but help but grow closer at the sight of her.

I wipe the fallen tear off of her cheek. "You looks so beautiful mi amor" I praise and look down to see her playing with herself and I moan feeling like I'm losing my mind over this woman.

"You're such a fucking slut for me Violette, playing with yourself while I use you like a fucktoy hm" she nods a little when I pull back watching the salvia connect from me to her lips a little going over her chin.

The scene in front of me is enough to make me come deep in her mouth. She swallows me like the good girl she is and I wipe the side of her mouth with my thumb which she takes between her lips.

"You drive me fucking insane" I wrap my hand around her neck and she smiles. I stand her up lifting her leg onto my hip, letting my tip run up and down her wet hot slit, she wraps her arms around my neck.

"Tell me you love me, I need to hear it" She whimpers slightly when I push myself inside.

"I love you Enzo, I will always love you" I rest my head on her shoulder letting the words drain into my head, words I never want to ever stop hearing.

I slowly move myself in and out of her while she continues to whisper the words that make my heart beat faster. Her nails slightly graze down my back, every inch of me was hers.

Violette had me wrapped around her finger since her brown eyes met my blue.

"I l-love you" She let's out while I continued to slowly pump myself into her, she always felt so perfect around me.

I use my hand around her neck so she looks at me. "Never stop saying those words to me, I need to hear them forever" her eyes threatened to close but she kept them on me.

"Never" she breathlessly said while I took her nipple in my mouth, her hands flowing freely through my hair. Her sounds only make me pick up my pace just to hear her call out my name louder.

"Come with me please Enzo" My angel calls out while I reach between us rubbing her swollen clit signaling her release faster.

—

"Why can't it be like this forever?" Violette says while we stand on the balcony watching the sunrise.

"It will be mi amore, I promise" I kiss the side of her cheek. She anxiously bites her lips and I ask her what's wrong.

"Enzo I need to tell you something" I begin to worry until her thumb strokes my cheek. "Tears weld her beautiful eyes and I press a kiss to her forehead telling her that it's okay.

"Boss, we've found him" Damien enters and Violette quickly shuts her mouth.

"No it's okay go, I'll tell you when you get back" I look for a sign that she's lying but I find none. She pulls me in for a kiss that leaves me wanting more as soon as she pulls away.

"Come back to me okay? I need you Enzo, we need you" she places a hand on her stomach and when I realizes tears begin to build and she nods her head.

I press one last kiss to her forehead and one to her stomach to the child I couldn't wait to meet and the woman I couldn't wait to marry. "I'll come back to you mi amore, to both of you"

She smiles and I can't help but want to hurry and end the life of the man who brought her so much pain.

"Father huh? Congratulations man" Mariano says giving me a pat on the back and it brings a smile on my face when I think about holding Violette's and I's child in my arms.

The feeling in my gut starts to pick up. "Something's wrong" Mariano checks the footage of Leonardo and he's just sitting in a warehouse tapping his finger on a watch. "Damien turn the fuck around"

The exact time Damien stops the car a loud beeping sound around us goes off.

The last thing I remember before everything went blurry was hearing Mariano's voice.

- so how is everyone doing?

- we don't have a lot of chapters before our stories come to an end.

- Taste Our Sins is out now chapters 1-5 hope to see you all there!

□ □ □ □ □ □

You're told parents are supposed to protect you from the world, allow you to grow and become better than they are. They isolate you from learning that the world is a scary place until you grow up and learn it for yourself.

I jump at the sound of footsteps stopping at the heavy door, when the code beeps my heart relaxing knowing only three people have that code. "Fuck, gorgeous are you okay?" Mariano pulls me into his arms and finally have time to breathe.

"I'm okay but you're bleeding" I point to his shirt and he grins.

"Not mine, we need to leave" I hold my stomach while he holds my hand running through the house.

I'm pregnant.

The thought of me being pregnant with Enzo's child calms me more, all he's ever wanted was to bring us nothing but peace and yet we were going through hell right now.

"Where is he?" I begin to worry more when Mariano doesn't say anything. "Mariano, where is he?" he curses at himself before stopping, pulling me to the side behind the wall, covering my mouth with his hand.

"Trust me on this, he's more than safe but I promised him that I would keep you safe. Take this" he places his favorite knife of his in my hands.

Two loud footsteps come forward and Mariano tells me to stay out before stepping out with his hands up. "Is this anyway to enter someone's home? No text, no phone call" he says to the two gentlemen.

"How's the little girl doing DelRosa? Still having nightmares?" his jaw clenches at the mention of Iris, but it turns into a sadistic smile. One I had never seen on Mariano only his playful smirk.

In a blink of my eyes, his hands hold two guns directly at their heads before pulling the trigger.

"All I wanted was to catch up" he stands over them both, he pats the bald ones cheek removing his gun.

"Don't be to upset, I'll be sure to give the wife a kiss goodnight" then he turns to me.

"Maybe write the kids a Christmas card that daddy's gone on a very long vacation."

Mariano drove past a car that seemed to have blown up and I noticed it's the same car they left in but it only had one body in it. "Don't worry it's not him" I nod calmly.

He drove into a dark warehouse before the lights turned on. He drives off going to go check on Iris.

Enzo was torturing a man with his white shirt filled with dirt and blood that wasn't his, his hair was drenched from sweat and there was only anger in his eyes. He yanked the guys hair back, repeatedly sending his fist into his abdomen.

He stuffed his gun in the man's mouth with a sinister grin. "Wrong answer" he finally said letting the bullet go.

You are not supposed to find this hot Violette. He just killed someone right in front of you.

But it's not the first time.

He unbuttons the bloody shirt, disposing of it. His back muscles tense before relaxing, the tattoos along his skin have always turned me on along with his abs.

Calm down, this is not the place of time for this.

Instead he turns to me, the anger dying when he sees that I'm okay. Then it returns at the sound of a gun-cocking at my head.

"Ultimatums seem to run in your family Romano" I fell my body freeze at the sound of my father's voice.

"What happened to Sophia was truly tragic, though I don't understand why she chose you over her. Why do they always chose you Enzo?" I clench my eyes shut when he pressed the gun to my back when Enzo points his gun at him but the two other men cock theirs at him.

"And my own daughter, isn't it funny how she would choose a man who's life would only have her end up dead at the end of the day" I try not to touch my stomach, if he knows I'm pregnant there's no doubt that he will kill me.

"Then she went to see her mother" he turns me around, his nails dig into my arm and I let out a shriek of pain. "The woman left you and you went running back to her, you really are a pathetic excuse of a daughter Violette"

When I don't say anything, he squeezes at my arm harder. "I'm going to fucking kill you" Enzo says behind me. Two men have their guns pointed at his head while his is on the floor.

I stare into my father's soulless brown eyes, nothing about them hold love or remorse for me.

"I'm just getting to know my daughter again" While his hands out in handcuff, the men besides Enzo begin punch him in his stomach, Enzo's groans fill my ears to the side of me and I can't help but feel that this is all my fault.

"I am not your daughter" I hiss when my knees hit the hard floor and faces me towards Enzo. His blue eyes plead with me to look away.

"What do you want from me?" I finally say and he smiles.

"I want nothing more than to see Enzo Romano left with nothing, and you're going to help me." he yanks my hair, forcefully making me watch.

I watch his eyes begin to slowly flow close and tears weld my eyes. "Please stop" he crouches down to me, grabbing my chin, his nails dig into my cheeks. Enzo's grunts fill my ears and I can't help but feel my heart shatter at the sound.

"I was left with nothing for years, then to my surprise my daughter was falling in love with the same man who took everything from me."

"It's simple really, all he has to do is chose between himself or you"

"You son of a"- Enzo's voice is cut off by a loud scream from his mouth.

"Why are you doing this?" It felt like a million sharp pieces of glass were piercing through my heart all at once watching Enzo take all of the torture.

"You don't get it, seeing him with nothing is all I need to die peacefully because there's no doubt that he's going to chose you then kill me. But as long as the love of his life is dead, I'll die a happy man" he taps the gun on my head.

"P-Please I'll do anything.. just stop hurting him" The lump in my throat begins to grow, the air in my lungs seem to be stuck.

"I won't hurt him, all you have to do is choose" he nudged me over to him pushing me forcefully on my knees.

"Violette I swear to fuck, don't you dare!" I hear him shout through the pain but I block his voice out but it only seems to fail.

I ignore the pin soaring through my knees, kneeling in front of Enzo, the men stop and only watch as I place my hands on his face.

"I'm so sorry" I say to Enzo. "I-I'm sorry" His face is bruised, a deep knife scar on his cheek. His body is now beaten, his once tanned skin is now covered in gashes and his blood.

"I-It's not your fault Violette, please don't do this" I lean my forehead on his, his tear slips from his face mixing with my own.

"I can't do this by myself mi amore please" He whispers to me only knowing I'm not going to kill him.

"I love you, you Enzo Aleksander Romano have my entire heart in your hands. Always have, Always will" My voice breaks and he shakes his head trying to break free from the cuffs but it only digs in his wrist more causing him pain.

I can't see him like this anymore.

"Promise me you won't stop loving me."

"I'm not going to fucking promise you that, I fucking love you Violette. Everything about you I've fallen deeply in love with. I'm not promising you shit because you aren't going to die" I cry harder, sniffling the tears and wiping his.

Placing a kiss to his cheek softly, then one to his forehead, lastly to his lips. "I won't forgive you if you do this" I hold his hands bound in front of him, curling them up into fist.

"F-Fuck Vio, please" My heart aches more at the sound of his voice breaking and I stand up mouthing a sorry to him.

I turn around to face my father, walking towards him until Enzo's voice stops me. "You promised"

"You promised not to lose me and you're breaking it, I gave you every fucking part of me. Every single part I never gave to the world, turn around and tell me you don't fucking care about me and I'll let you walk out with him."

I bite my trembling lip resisting the urge to hold my stomach. "Violette we don't have time for this" my father says.

"My body is yours, every breathe I take belongs to you, my heart, my soul, my tears. Tesoro it's all yours" My father places the gun in my hands and I clutch it trying to drain out his words.

"I wasn't supposed to fall for you but dammit how couldn't I? Every time I hear laugh, see your smile, feel your touch. I forget every bad moment in my life, every stab wound in my heart is fixed every time I look at you."

The sound of his cuffs fall and Enzo grabs the gun tucked between behind him and shoots the two guys in the head, my father grabs me holding a knife to my neck making him rage with anger.

"After you Enzo, there's no more left. The moment your blood pours on the floor, everything you're pathetic family ever built will die to the ground along with you" I use my right hand to fight against his hold on my neck, sneaking my left hand underneath my dress to pull out Mariano's knife.

"And if I die, at least I can take my daughter with me right?" he pressed the metal a little harder.

"Stop calling me that!" I jam the knife into his thigh and he drops his falling to his knee.

"I'm not your fucking daughter, you aren't my father. You are nothing to me" I hold the gun directly at him and he smiles.

"You aren't a killer Violette, but for him I guess you would live with the fact you took someone's life right? You'll live with the constant reminder of my blood on your hands, every time you sleep this moment will forever play in your head right?" My hands begin to shake and I can't breathe.

"She was born a killer and I'd be dammed if I ever let her go through what I have. She isn't a killer but I am" Enzo grips his hair placing the gun at his heart and I back away as the sound of the bullet courses through my ears.

I look away from the scene of his lifeless body collapsing forbidding him from ever haunting me again. I feel his strong arms come around me and hold me dearly not letting me slip away from him.

"Please don't ever do that again, I-I thought you were going to leave me. I thought I had actually lost you, both of you" he slightly caresses my stomach in the deep embrace.

"Please tell me it's over Enzo" I close my eyes sealing them shut, my heart hurts, my body is in shock and my brain is pounding against my skull.

"It's over tesoro, I promise" I sob into his neck and he ignores the pain of his body holding me tightly.

The pain, the love, the torment of knowing nothing good would come from us being happy with each other wasn't enough to keep either one of us away.

The sea of those blue eyes had me since the first day I stepped foot on the stage, the first time my body touched his.

In the end we were chaos to each other in many ways, my eyes were his storm, his smile was my peace. In one he found his life's meaning in brown eyes, tears frozen cold fell onto his soft cheeks, holding my body in his arms, our once cold bodies now engulfing in each other's warmth.

"No more chaos mi amore" he lifts my head, staring into my eyes. "No more."

- the end -

* not edited *

- chapter thoughts?

- book thoughts?

- epilogue will be out soon!

- I love every single one of you that stuck around to the end, silent and vocal readers.

- kisses

- Rose

EPILOGUE

"Iris slow down!" Emilio called out, while Mariano paid for her ice-cream.

She ran into his leg holding tightly, the ten year old girl took her strawberry cone. "Can we please go up there?" she pointed to the tall building next to the Eiffel Tower.

"You've had to much sugar, little flower. Are you sure you want to?" she nodded her head, pouting at her father knowing he couldn't resist it.

"It's Milio's fault! He bought me more candy before we came here" she pointed to her uncle who had his jaw dropped.

"That was supposed to be a secret!" Mariano rose an eyebrow at his younger brother who was now avoiding his gaze at all times.

Mariano took the strawberry cone from his daughter making her lip quiver. "You need real food first, I'll buy you another one hm?" she nodded with a sad pout taking her father's hand before throwing a scowl at her uncle.

Emilio was now eighteen, decided to move to Paris with Mariano made him happier. Mariano promised them both they would travel the world.

They continued up the large elevator, Iris smiled brightly at the beautiful view only enlightening a smile to Mariano's face that he could make his daughter smile.

Taking a seat at the large restaurant, Emilio and Iris fought like children over which dessert they wanted to settle on and Mariano could only sit back and laugh.

Getting up to the restroom, he bumped into a familiar figure. "Beautiful?" he greeted. Grace had simply worn a white silk dress which fell to her thighs, her figure was simply breathtaking.

Even then she couldn't forget those freckles and green eyes which held mischief. "Mr. Delrosa" she smiled softly at the taller man.

"You look.. beautiful" Mariano mentally face palmed himself at the feeling of his face heating up.

"Thank you" Grace found the tint on his cheeks adorable to her.

"I should get back to my husband" Mariano's face fell, he turned to the man she pointed at.

"Seth? Seth is your husband?" She furrowed her eyebrows, wondering how he knew her husband's name.

"Baby?" Her husband came behind them only to meet the face of Mariano and cleared his throat.

"Do you two know each other?" Mariano smirked down at Grace who began to fiddle with her purse.

"I'm an old friend" Mariano couldn't stop thinking about the night they shared before he left to Paris, last thing he expected was to see her here, married.

The thought angered him, he missed her lips. Her lips on his body, her lips on his. How soft her skin was on his, how good she looked underneath and on top of him.

"I think we should get going, it was nice seeing you again Mariano" the sound of his name falling from her tongue seemed to only make his situation in his pants worse.

"Until next time beautiful" Grace almost let her jaw drop at how blunt he was in front of her husband.

It was simply because he didn't care.

—

"Enzo stop" Violette pleads her husband, Enzo begins to place his lips on her neck, leaving the mark of his love for her on her soft skin.

The moonlight rained on the married couple as the sound of her angelic laughs filled his ears.

"Mhm, tell me you love me again" Violette closed her legs around him, biting her lip until a light smack is placed on her ass, she pushes him lightly.

Holding his face in her hands, she can't help but fall in love the more she sees him. "I love you" Enzo's smile deepens, even after four years. He isn't over the three words that fall from her perfect lips. His black hair was a tad longer, falling over his face just how she liked it. His eyes seemed to glow every time they looked at her with his captivating and teasing smile.

A tiny knock came to the door and Enzo sat up against the headboard before there son ran in a hurry, climbing on the bed in between his parents.

Violette smoothed his black curls from his face staring into his panicked eyes, the blue one resembling Enzo's and the brown one matching Violette's. "What's wrong mi amore?" she asked Mateo who began to cuddle his way into her chest.

"N-Nightmare" he whispered while Enzo soothed his back up and down. Mateo shut his eyes trying to calm his breathing. "Y-You both left me, I was scared" he sniffled, burying his face deeper.

Enzo lifted their son onto his lap, he played with his fingers. "We're right here, we aren't going anywhere mi amore" Violette said placing a kiss to his chubby cheek making him smile.

"Promise" he held out his pinky to the both of them, connecting their fingers the promised.

"Can I sleep here please?" he pouted his lips and his eyes began to grow sad. "I promise to cuddle both of you" he happily sat between them when they agreed to his offer.

Placing a kiss to his father's cheek, then to his mother's. Mateo fell asleep within seconds without another nightmare that night.

"I love you Mrs. Romano" Enzo said quietly leaning over his son to kiss Violette. Biting her lip gently as a tease until letting it go, Violette held the side of his face only to deepen the kiss.

"My tesoro?" He stared into her eyes, the same ones that had him in the palm of her hands at first glance. "Your Tesoro" she responded before they placed their lips back together, then one of either side of their son's face.

The kiss they wanted forever.

- we've officially made it to the end of CHAOS.

- Thank you to all the silent and vocal readers .

- book thoughts ?

This is where I let you go.

And before you say you love me more.

It's not possible because I love you way more

- One last kiss for this book.

- Taste Our Sins is out now !!

- Rose

www.ingramcontent.com/pod-product-compliance
Lightning Source LLC
LaVergne TN
LVHW050800061126
851857LV00012B/623
* 9 7 8 3 7 2 5 5 6 4 5 0 7 *